The King's Fund

Ideas that change health care

Transforming the delivery of health and social care

The case for fundamental change

Authors
Chris Ham
Anna Dixon
Beatrice Brooke

›Time to Think Differently

The King's Fund seeks to understand how the health system in England can be improved. Using that insight, we help to shape policy, transform services and bring about behaviour change. Our work includes research, analysis, leadership development and service improvement. We also offer a wide range of resources to help everyone working in health to share knowledge, learning and ideas.

Published by
The King's Fund
11–13 Cavendish Square
London W1G 0AN
Tel: 020 7307 2591
Fax: 020 7307 2801
www.kingsfund.org.uk

First published 2012 by The King's Fund

Charity registration number: 1126980

ISBN: 978 1 909029 00 2

A catalogue record for this publication is available from the British Library

Available from:
The King's Fund
11–13 Cavendish Square
London W1G 0AN
Tel: 020 7307 2591
Fax: 020 7307 2801
Email: publications@kingsfund.org.uk
www.kingsfund.org.uk/publications

Edited by Giovanna Ceroni

Typeset by Grasshopper Design Company

Printed in the UK by The King's Fund

It is time to think differently about health and social care. The health and social care system in England faces unprecedented funding pressures and is underpinned by a delivery model that is not fit to meet the challenges of the future. We are undertaking a programme of work that looks at the medium- to longer-term drivers of change to support leaders in health and social care in their decision-making.

We will assess the long-term funding requirements for health and social care and explain why we believe current models of care are unlikely to deliver the transformation in services needed. By engaging others and stimulating debate, we hope to generate new thinking about innovative ways of delivering high-quality care that meet the needs of the population and offer value for money.

We hope you will join us and take time to think differently about the future of health and social care. For more information, go to www.kingsfund.org.uk/change

Contents

List of figures and tables

About the authors

Chris Ham took up his post as Chief Executive of The King's Fund in April 2010. He has been professor of health policy and management at the University of Birmingham, England, since 1992. From 2000 to 2004 he was seconded to the Department of Health where he was director of the strategy unit, working with ministers on NHS reform. Chris is the author of 20 books and numerous articles about health policy and management.

Chris has advised the World Health Organization and the World Bank and has served as a consultant to governments in a number of countries. He is an honorary fellow of the Royal College of Physicians of London and of the Royal College of General Practitioners, an honorary professor at the London School of Hygiene and Tropical Medicine, a companion of the Institute of Healthcare Management and a visiting professor at the University of Surrey. In 2004 he was awarded a CBE for his services to the NHS.

Anna Dixon is Director of Policy at The King's Fund. She has conducted research and published widely on health care funding and policy. She has given lectures on a range of topics including UK health system reform and patient choice. She was previously a lecturer in European Health Policy at the London School of Economics and was awarded the Commonwealth Fund Harkness Fellowship in Health Care Policy in 2005/6. Anna has also worked in the Strategy Unit at the Department of Health, where she focused on a range of issues including choice, global health and public health.

Beatrice Brooke joined The King's Fund in January 2012 as Policy and Research Adviser to the Chief Executive. She was previously Policy Manager at the British Heart Foundation, working on a policy portfolio spanning prevention, treatment and care of heart disease. Before this, she worked at the Royal College of Paediatrics and Child Health and at the Department of Health. While on the NHS General Management Graduate Training Scheme, Beatrice worked in both operational and strategic NHS management. Beatrice holds a Masters in Healthcare Leadership and Management from the universities of Birmingham and Manchester.

Acknowledgements

The authors are grateful for contributions and comments by a number of colleagues, including Richard Bohmer in relation to innovation, Angela Coulter on the role of patients, Penny Dash and Nigel Edwards for comments on an early draft, Amy Galea and James Thompson for help in tracking down facts and figures, Richard Humphries for comments on social care, Candace Imison for comments on successive drafts and Chris Naylor on mental health. We alone are responsible for the final version of the paper.

Summary

Major progress has been made in improving the performance of the NHS in the past decade. Notwithstanding this progress, the current health and social care delivery system has failed to keep pace with the needs of an ageing population, the changing burden of disease, and rising patient and public expectations. Fundamental change to the delivery system is needed, with greater emphasis on:

- preventing illness and tackling risk factors, such as obesity, to help people remain in good health
- supporting people to live in their own homes and offering a wider range of housing options in the community
- providing high standards of primary care in all practices to enable more services to be delivered in primary care, where appropriate
- making more effective use of community health services and related social care, and ensuring these services are available 24/7 when needed
- using acute hospitals and care homes only for those people who cannot be treated or cared for more appropriately in other settings
- integrating care around the needs of people and populations.

The fact that on some indicators the NHS appears to do better than other systems does not undermine our contention that fundamental change is required. We believe that all systems need to adapt rapidly to changing population needs, regardless of how well they perform.

Evidence that the current health and social care delivery system is broken and requires radical reform includes the following.

- Variations in health outcomes between social groups persist and in some cases are widening (Marmot 2010).
- The United Kingdom has the second highest rate of mortality amenable to health care among 16 high-income nations, despite recent falls in death rates (Nolte and McKee 2011).
- 10,000 lives would be saved each year if England achieved cancer survival rates at the level of the European best (Department of Health 2011a).
- 24,000 people with diabetes die each year from avoidable causes related to their condition, and £170 million could be saved each year through better understanding and management (National Audit Office 2012).
- As many as 1,500 children a year might not die if the United Kingdom performed as well as Sweden in relation to illnesses that rely on first-access care, such as asthma and pneumonia (Wolfe *et al* 2011).

- Variations in the quality of general practice show that in the lowest performing practices only around a quarter of patients report being able to see their preferred doctor, and only 11 per cent of patients report that they have been told they have a care plan (The King's Fund 2011).
- Three-quarters of people with depression and anxiety receive no treatment, and the extra physical health care caused by mental illness costs the NHS at least £10 billion each year (London School of Economics and Political Science 2012).
- Around one in 10 hospital admissions results in some form of harm (House of Commons Health Committee 2009).
- There is excess mortality in hospitals at weekends (Dr Foster Intelligence 2011), and in London alone there would be a minimum of 500 fewer deaths a year if the weekend mortality rate was the same as the weekday rate (NHS London 2011).
- Lives could be saved and quality of life improved by the concentration of some specialist services such as stroke and vascular surgery in fewer hospitals (Naylor R *et al* 2012). In London an estimated 400 lives will be saved each year through the designation of eight hyper-acute stroke units (Nicholson 2012).
- More than half of 100 acute hospitals inspected by the Care Quality Commission in 2011 were non-compliant with standards of dignity and nutrition for older people, or were found to give cause for concern (Care Quality Commission 2011).
- More than four-fifths (85 per cent) of local authorities restrict publicly funded care to those with substantial and/or critical needs (Association of Directors of Adult Social Services 2012).
- The stock of specialist housing for older people will need to grow by 40–70 per cent over the next 20 years (Pannell *et al* 2012).

Unprecedented funding pressures affecting health and social care mean that incremental changes to current models of care will not be sufficient to address these and other challenges. A much bolder approach is needed, involving a major shift in where care is delivered and how patients and service users relate to health and social care professionals.

In our view, the future health and social care delivery system needs to:

- see patients and service users as part of the care team
- focus on the development of effective health and social care teams in which staff work flexibly and full use is made of the range of skills available
- provide care in the right place at the right time by reducing overreliance on hospitals and care homes
- use information and communication technologies to revolutionise patients' and users' experiences
- harness the potential of new medical technologies more effectively
- make intelligent use of data and information to empower patients and support professionals to deliver high-quality care.

These radical changes to the delivery system will become a reality only if the implementation of new models of care is given serious attention. This will involve decommissioning outdated models of care to create resources and space for new ones to emerge; supporting NHS organisations to innovate and adopt established best practices; and making it easier for new providers to enter the market where this is appropriate. Attitudes towards risk-taking need to change to support the transformation of the delivery system and to actively encourage experimentation. Leaders at a local level have a major part to play in translating the ideas discussed in this paper into practice.

Introduction

> *We have to strive to alter our whole mentality about hospitals... Hospital building is not like pyramid building, the erection of memorials to endure to a remote posterity. We have to get the idea into our heads that a hospital is a shell, a framework, however complex, to contain certain processes, and when processes change or are superseded, then the shell must most probably be scrapped and the framework dismantled.*
>
> Enoch Powell

As a result of the changes contained in the Health and Social Care Act 2012, the NHS is implementing one of the most radical reorganisations in its history. These changes are dominated by the abolition of old organisations such as primary care trusts and strategic health authorities, and the creation of new structures such as clinical commissioning groups and health and wellbeing boards. The architecture of the NHS at a national level is also being reshaped through the establishment of the NHS Commissioning Board and the 're-invention' of Monitor as a sector regulator.

In our view the reforms embedded in the Health and Social Care Act 2012 fail to address the longer-term underlying trends and pressures affecting health and social care services. This is due to the fact that these reforms are mainly concerned with how the NHS is organised, rather than how care is delivered. Different and more fundamental changes are needed to the provision of health and social care services if they are to be fit for the future. This paper makes the case for fundamental change, drawing on evidence and examples from a wide variety of sources.

Although we acknowledge the many improvements in quality and outcomes that have occurred in recent years, we believe that the ageing population and increased prevalence of long-term conditions require a sea change in thinking and action that goes well beyond arguments about how to improve the performance of the existing system. The current reliance on care in hospitals and residential settings is increasingly and rightly under question, as are traditional relationships between health and social care professionals and service users. Evidence of gaps in quality and safety in the NHS underscore the urgent need to develop new models of care.

Our argument echoes that of the seminal analysis carried out by the Institute of Medicine in the United States in *Crossing the Quality Chasm* (Committee on Quality of Health Care in America, Institute of Medicine 2001) and underlines the point that the health care systems of high-income countries around the world are faced with similar challenges. The health and social care delivery system is too focused on dealing with yesterday's challenges rather than those of tomorrow. New thinking is needed both on the models of care required in the future and on how these are to be put in place.

The proximate cause of the pressures affecting health and social care services is the prospect of many years of financial constraints on public expenditure. In the case of the NHS, these constraints require around £20 billion of efficiency savings to be found by 2015, with a high probability that a similar amount will need to be identified in the following four years (Appleby 2012). Social care is under even greater pressure with local authorities having to make deep cuts in spending. In the absence of additional funding to develop new services, the challenge facing local authorities and NHS organisations is how to use the resources available now and for the foreseeable future to meet the demands of the populations they serve.

The current delivery model in all providers (hospitals, primary care, community services, social care and mental health) is based on outdated ways of working that result in poor value for money and lack of user responsiveness. If the productivity challenges that lie ahead are to be met, a major transformation in care delivery is required. As we have argued before, 'salami-slicing' of budgets and incremental adjustments to existing services will not be sufficient to deliver the changes that are needed (Appleby *et al* 2010). All of those involved in commissioning and delivering health and social care services must look beyond current models of care to create a delivery system that really is fit for the future.

Radical changes would be needed even if the current funding pressures affecting health and social care did not exist. The ageing population and increased prevalence of long-term conditions and multi-morbidity raise major questions about how health and social care services are organised and delivered. In particular, the separation between general practitioners (GPs) and hospital-based specialists, and between health and social care often inhibit the provision of timely and high-quality integrated care to people who need to access a range of services relevant to their needs. Furthermore, evidence presented in this report of variations in the quality of care and the opportunities that exist to improve outcomes and save money provide a compelling case for change.

Current models of care also appear to be outmoded at a time when society and technologies are evolving rapidly and are changing the way in which we interact with each other and with service providers. While health and social care services have evolved since the establishment of the NHS, change has been much slower than in other industries such as banking and retailing, where the use of technology has transformed the relationship between service providers and their customers. Experience in other countries where health care organisations have already embraced new technologies indicates the shape of things to come and the potential to deliver care more effectively.

This paper therefore stands back from discussions of current policies to assess the major drivers of change and the implications for the future. In our opinion, national and local leaders must take a strategic view rather than focusing on short-term fixes designed to preserve existing services at a time when these are in need of more radical reform. A strategic view must start by understanding changes in need and demand, and how these affect the provision of services.

We begin by focusing on demographic pressures, the shifting burden of disease and disability, trends in health and lifestyle behaviours, and changing public and patient expectations. We also discuss a number of supply-side drivers, including medical advances and the availability of financial and human resources and how these might impact on the future delivery of health and social care services. As part of our programme of work we have conducted a more comprehensive analysis of underlying trends; the results of this analysis will be published later in 2012.

We then move on to review whether current models of delivering care are fit for purpose, drawing on evidence from different sources to make the case for change. We consider the delivery of public health and preventive services, primary care, hospital services, social care and mental health services. Our core argument here is that these services have not kept pace with changing demands. We also argue that they remain fragmented and fail to act together to meet the needs of patients and users. Recent scandals, including the failings of care at Mid Staffordshire NHS Foundation Trust and Winterbourne View, underline the need for change in all parts of the current system.

Having made the case for change, we go on to consider where the opportunities for innovation might lie. We consider the role of the patients and users in service design and delivery, professional roles and skill-mix, the location of care, the use of information and communication technologies, the opportunities presented by medical advances, the potential of data and information and how this could be harnessed for transformations in care. These issues are discussed at a high level and will be followed through in greater detail in subsequent work.

Many of the ideas in this paper have been outlined by others before us, yet the health and social care system has been slow to change. If the arguments set out here are to make a difference, then transformative leadership will be needed at all levels with greater support for risk-taking and experimentation, and acceptance that failure is sometimes the price to be paid for innovation. It will also be important to find more effective ways of decommissioning existing services that are no longer fit for purpose to create space for new models to emerge. We outline our thinking on these issues in the final part of the paper.

In making the case for changes to the delivery system, it is important to emphasise the many strengths of the NHS and the need to retain and build on these. Specifically, the commitment to universal access to care, the provision of a comprehensive range of services, and the ability to focus on the needs of the whole population are widely acknowledged to be enduring features that must be protected and wherever possible enhanced. The argument for a fundamental review of how care is currently provided is based on our assessment that radical changes in service models are needed if these core strengths are to be sustained.

It is also important to emphasise that the critique outlined here is of the system in which care is delivered, rather than of the staff working in the system. Our belief is that people who choose to work in health and social care are strongly motivated to provide the best possible care to patients and service users but are often frustrated in their ability to do so. Constant restructuring of the health and social care system focused on organisational changes not only misses the point that improvements in services are what matters, but also make it difficult for those working in the system to deliver high-quality care in line with their training and values.

This paper is the first in a series of outputs from a programme of work by The King's Fund during 2012–13 on the future of health and social care. It aims to establish the case for change and to stimulate thinking and debate about how models of care and service delivery need to develop in future. It does not seek to provide comprehensive or detailed answers, but rather sets out some of the current thinking about where future solutions might lie.

Through this programme of work, we aim to challenge assumptions and create an opportunity for policy-makers and leaders of the health and social care system to think differently. We hope our work will stimulate those leading health and social care organisations at all levels to engage in more radical and longer-term thinking. We also hope that they will be inspired to lead change in order to create a delivery system that is sustainable and rises to the challenges of the future.

1 The drivers of change

Today's health and social care services are built on the foundations of the needs of the post-war population they were set up to serve. These services have evolved over the past 60 years and must continue to adapt in response to a number of drivers of change. In this section, we summarise the nature of these drivers and assess their implications for the health and social care system of the future.

Demographic changes

The population of England has increased from 41 million in 1951 (Hawe *et al* 2011) to 53 million in 2012, and on current projections will reach 61 million by 2032 (Office for National Statistics 2011a). Population increases have been accompanied by a rise in the number of people aged 65 and over, and a change in the balance between people in this age group and those of working age.

The old-age dependency ratio – defined as the number of people of pension age and over for every 1,000 people of working age – demonstrates these changes in the structure of the population. Were there no increases in pension age, the ratio in the United Kingdom would increase from around 300 in 2006 to 375 in 2021 and 492 in 2051. Even taking into account the planned changes in pension age, the ratio will stand at 358 in 2041 and 342 in 2051 (Office for National Statistics 2012).

Increases in the number of 'older old' are particularly important. The number of people aged 85 and over in England rose from 416,000 in 1971 to over 1.1 million in 2009, and is projected to rise to over 2.6 million in 2032 (Office for National Statistics 2011a). The number of people living to 100 years or over is also on the rise from 1,080 in England and Wales in 1970 to 11,610 in 2010, and is estimated to exceed 160,000 across the United Kingdom by 2040 (Office for National Statistics 2011c).

Figure 1, opposite, illustrates the projected change in the age structure of the population in the United Kingdom over the next 20 years.

While increased longevity is a cause for celebration, it has implications for health and social care services. The main users of hospitals and care homes today are older people. As an example, people over 65 account for 62 per cent of total bed days in hospitals in England, and 68 per cent of emergency bed days (Imison *et al* 2012). Average length of stay in hospital is eight days for patients aged 65–74 years; 10 days for patients aged 75–84 years; and 12 days for patients aged 85 years or older (Cornwell *et al* 2012). More than three-quarters of people receiving care in registered residential and nursing accommodation in England funded by councils are aged 65 and over (with 43 per cent aged 85 and over), and 81 per cent of people receiving community-based home-care services are aged 65 or over (NHS Information Centre 2012).

Figure 1 Age distribution of the population of the United Kingdom, actual (2010) and projected (2035)

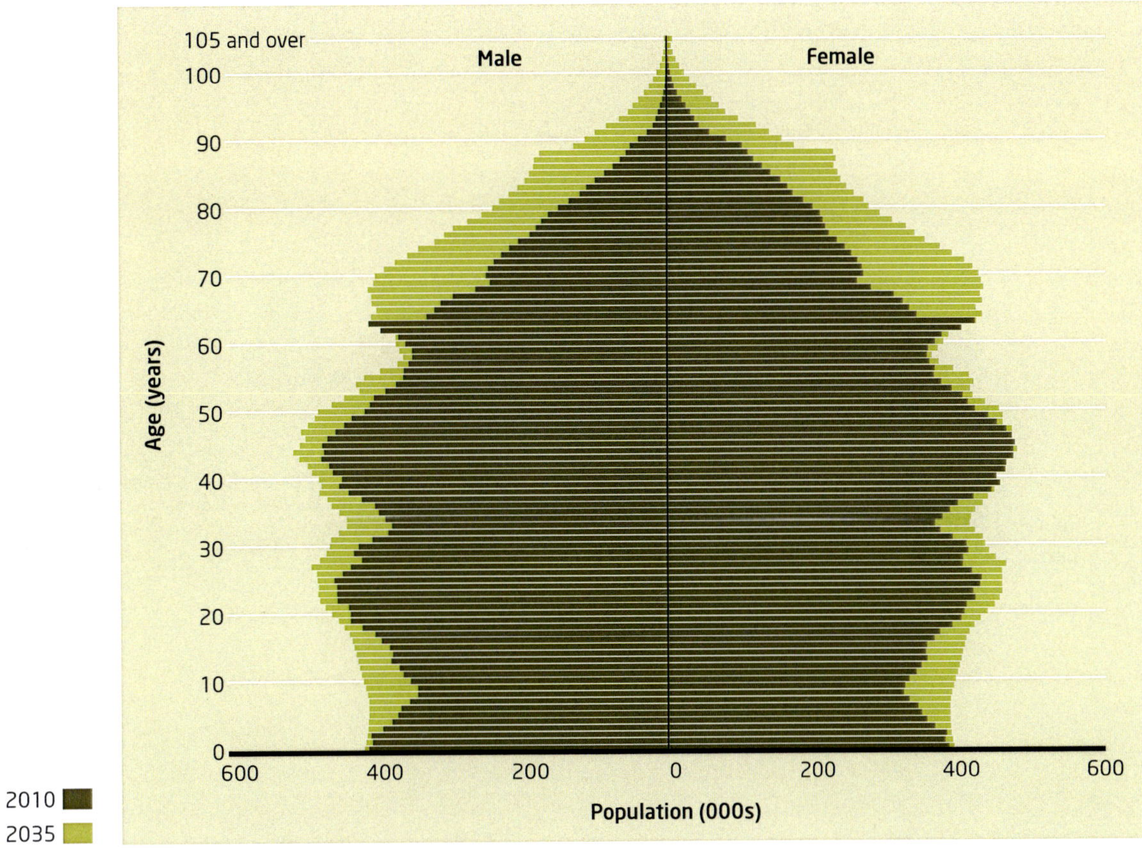

Source: Office for National Statistics (2011a)

The ageing population has resulted in rising demand for and use of health services. This is illustrated in Figure 2, below, which shows how the number of elective and non-elective hospital admissions in the past 20 years has increased much more rapidly than the growth in population. In the next section we discuss evidence on the opportunities that exist to provide more care in settings other than hospitals and care homes in future.

Figure 2 Increases in population by age and in elective and non-elective hospital admissions (%), England 1989/90–2009/10

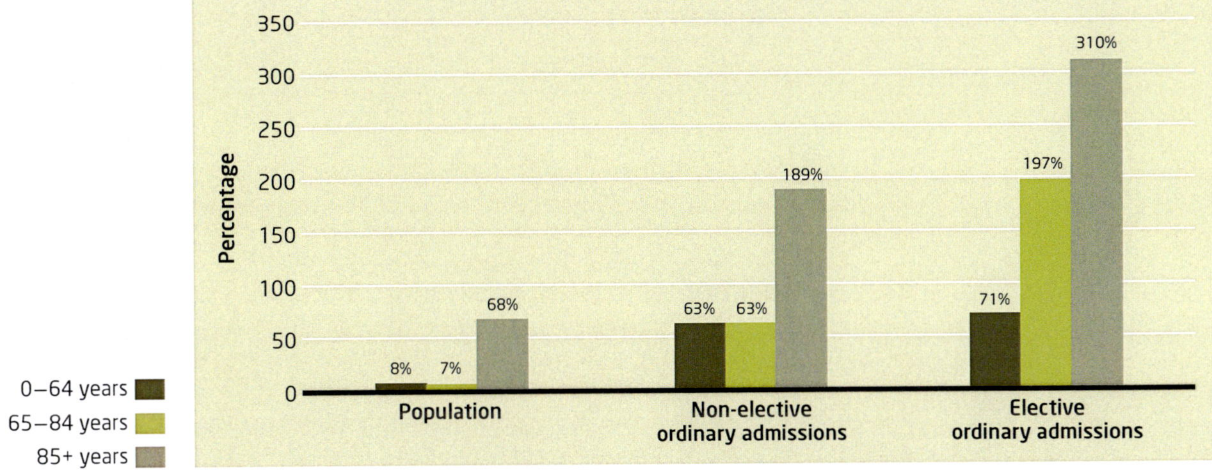

Source: The King's Fund analysis of HES data and Office for National Statistics (2011e)

Figure 3 Annual cost* by age and service area for Torbay (population 145,000), 2010/11

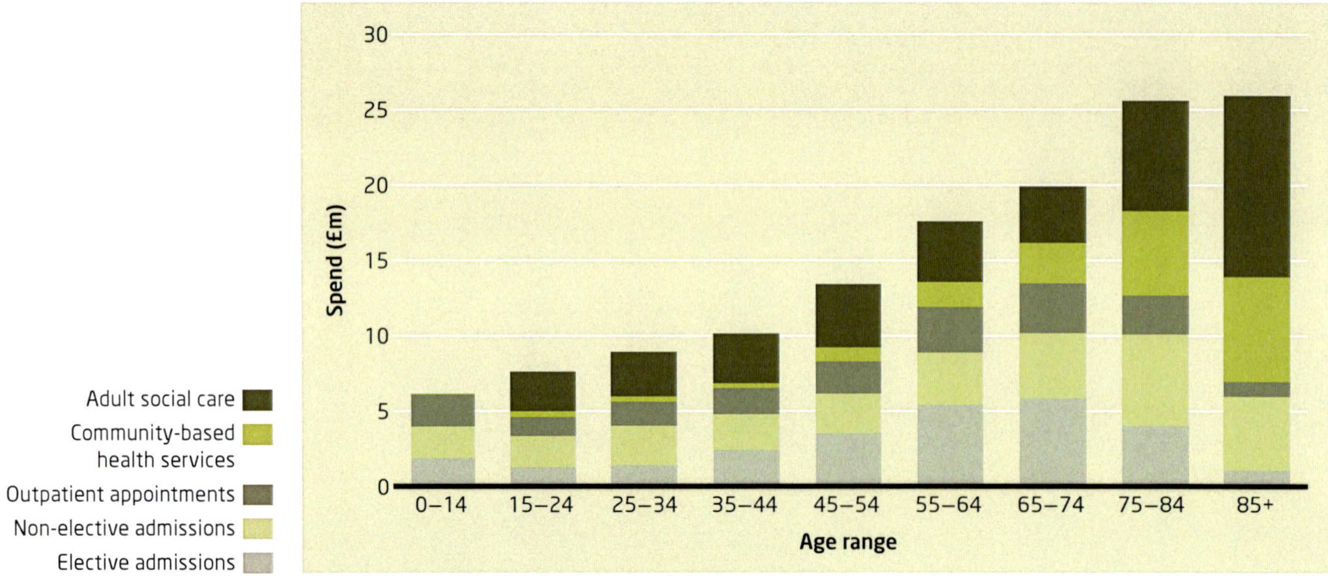

*Costs of primary care and prescribing are not included

Source: Torbay Care Trust (reproduced with permission)

Figure 3, above, provides an example of how health and social care spending increases with age and the different elements of this spending. Of particular note is the increase in spending on social care with age, especially among people aged 85 and over.

> **The proportion of the population who are old or very old is rising and so too are demands on health and social care. The health and social care system has not adapted to meet the needs of the growing number of older people and there is too great a reliance on hospitals and care homes.**

Health outcomes and life expectancy

In England and Wales, a boy born in 1948 could expect to live to the age of 65.9 years and a girl to the age of 70.3 years (Office for National Statistics 2011f). By 2010, the figures for England only were 77.8 years for boys and 82.9 years for girls. By 2032, life expectancy at birth in England is expected to increase to 83.3 years for men and 86.8 years for women (Office for National Statistics 2011b).

Life expectancy has also increased for people in retirement. In England and Wales in 1948, a man aged 65 could expect to live an additional 12.6 years and a woman an additional 15 years (Office for National Statistics 2011f). By 2010 in England the figures were 18.3 years for men and 20.9 years for women. By 2032, life expectancy at 65 is expected to increase to 22.0 years for men and 24.4 years for women (Office for National Statistics 2011b).

Increases in life expectancy have resulted from reductions in premature deaths from major causes such as heart disease, strokes, cancers and respiratory disease, as shown in Figure 4, opposite.

As life expectancy increases, a critical question is whether the years of life gained will be spent in health or illness. Figure 5, opposite, shows an increase in years of ill health among people aged 65 and over in the period 1981–2006, with a clearer trend for men

Figure 4 Leading causes of mortality for major diseases for males and females (age-standardised rates per million population), United Kingdom, 1971–2009

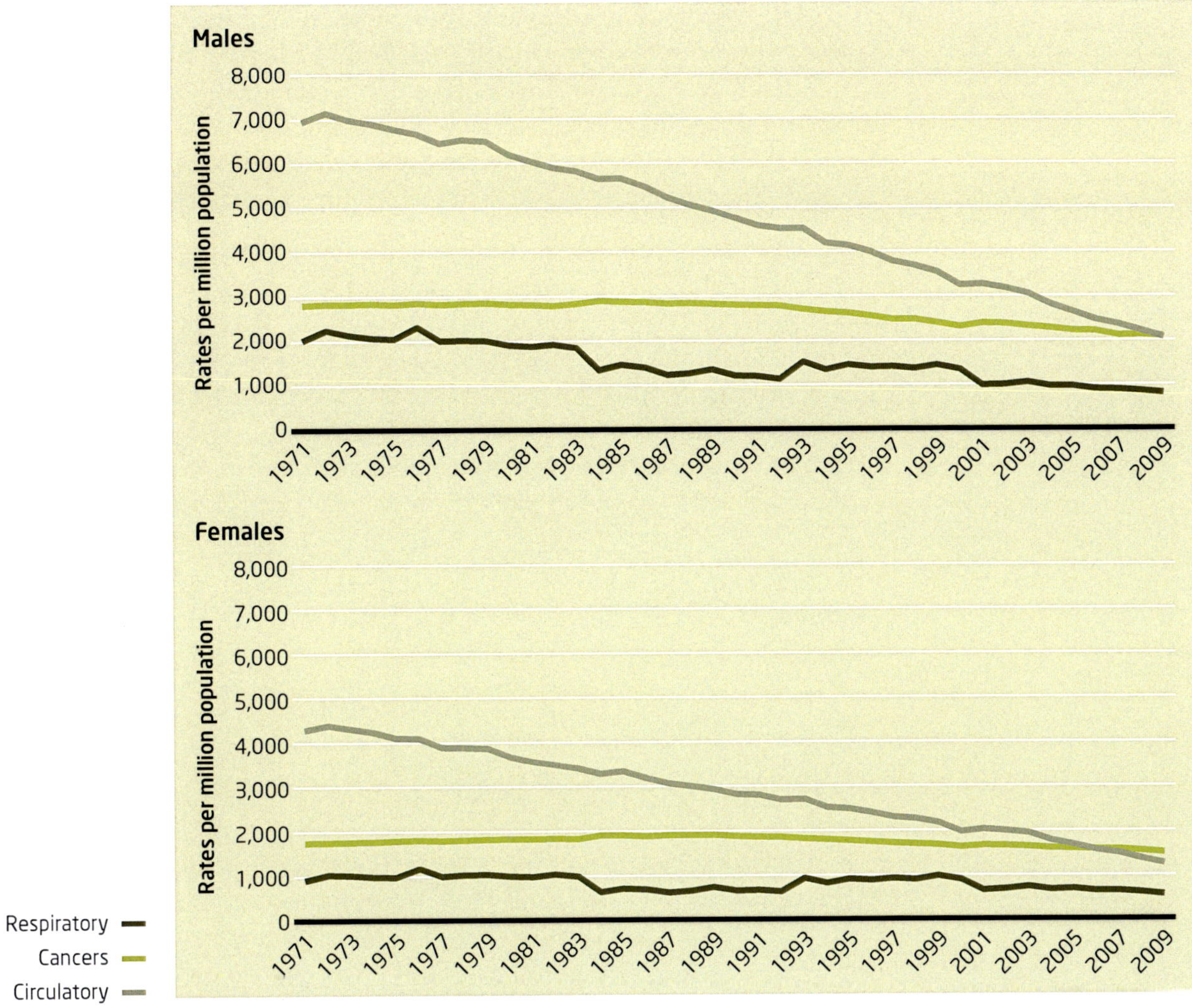

Source: Office for National Statistics (2011f)

Figure 5 Life expectancy, self-reported healthy life expectancy and years of ill health in people aged 65, England, 1981–2006*

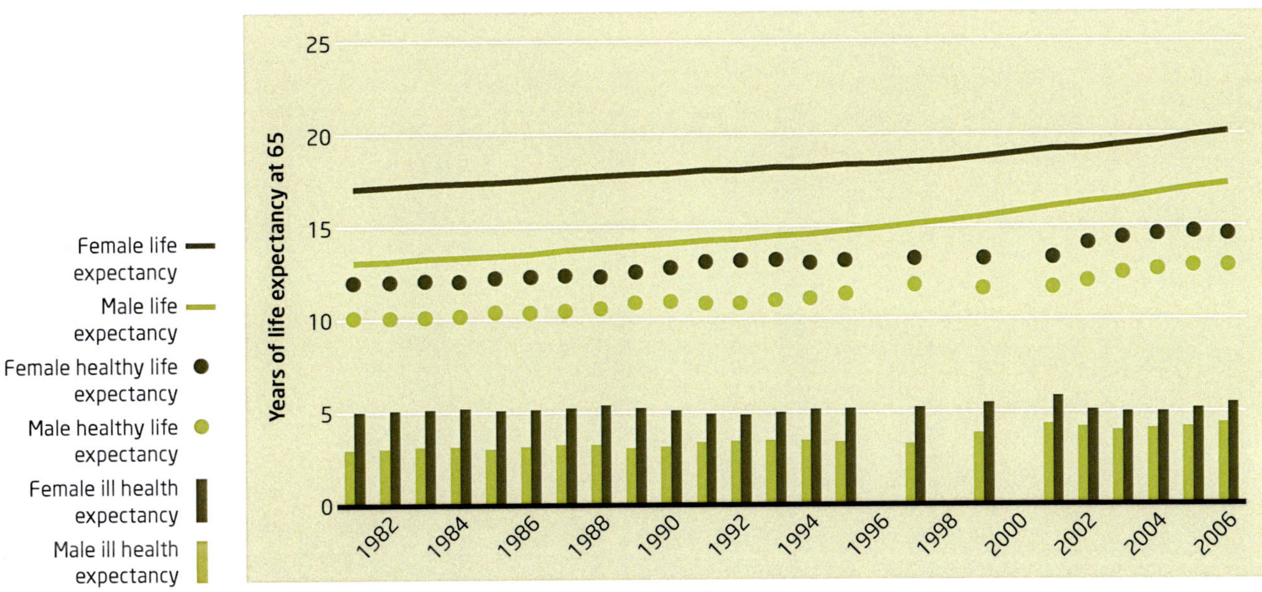

Source: Office for National Statistics (2004, 2011d)

* Data unavailable for 1996, 1998, 2000

than women. This may reflect the increased prevalence of long-term conditions, including dementia and other mental health problems, as discussed further below.

There is no consensus on whether in future there will be an expansion or compression of morbidity (more or fewer years spent in ill health) either for England or internationally, partly because conflicting influences are at work. While medical advances could postpone or limit the impact of ageing, risk factors like obesity may increase the number of years spent in ill health. This uncertainty means that it is also difficult to assess whether increased life expectancy postpones or increases the costs of ageing.

While there have been improvements in health across the social spectrum, there has been no narrowing of the gap between rich and poor despite several attempts over the years to tackle health inequalities, and there is some evidence of the gap widening (Marmot 2010). Inequalities in health apply at all ages and result from deep-seated social, economic and cultural determinants, as well as from behaviour and lifestyle factors. As Figure 6, below, shows, at age 16, living in the most deprived neighbourhoods in England reduces length of life by 7.6 years on average for men and 5.3 years for women, and the time spent living free of disability by around 13 years for men and women (Smith *et al* 2011).

Health outcomes have improved as a result of reductions in premature deaths from leading causes such as heart disease, strokes and cancers. While life expectancy has increased for both men and women, the number of years spent in ill health has also increased. Persistent and in some cases widening inequalities in health pose a major challenge.

The burden of disease and disability

Medical advances have turned many life-threatening conditions such as some cancers and heart disease into long-term conditions, as more people survive acute episodes of illness and live many years with their conditions. This helps to explain why the additional

Figure 6 Life expectancy and disability-free life expectancy at age 16*, by level of deprivation, men and women, England, 2006–8

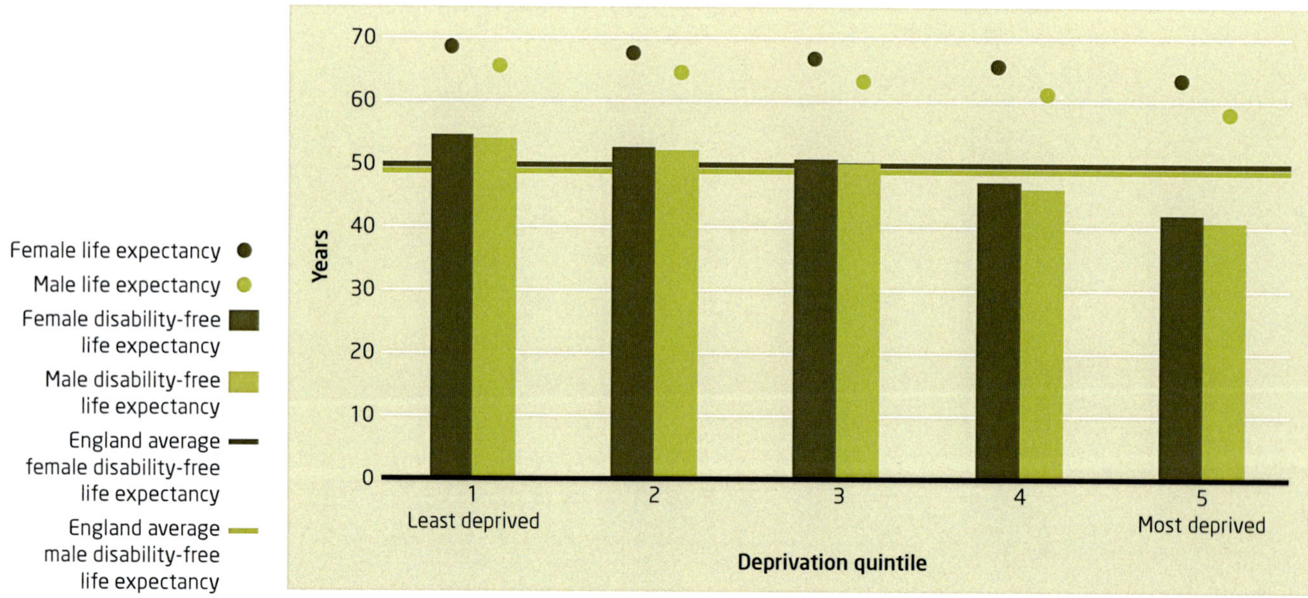

*Excludes residents of communal establishments except NHS housing and students in halls of residence where inclusion takes place at their parents' address

Source: Smith *et al* (2011)

Figure 7 Proportion of people with long-term conditions by age, England, 2009

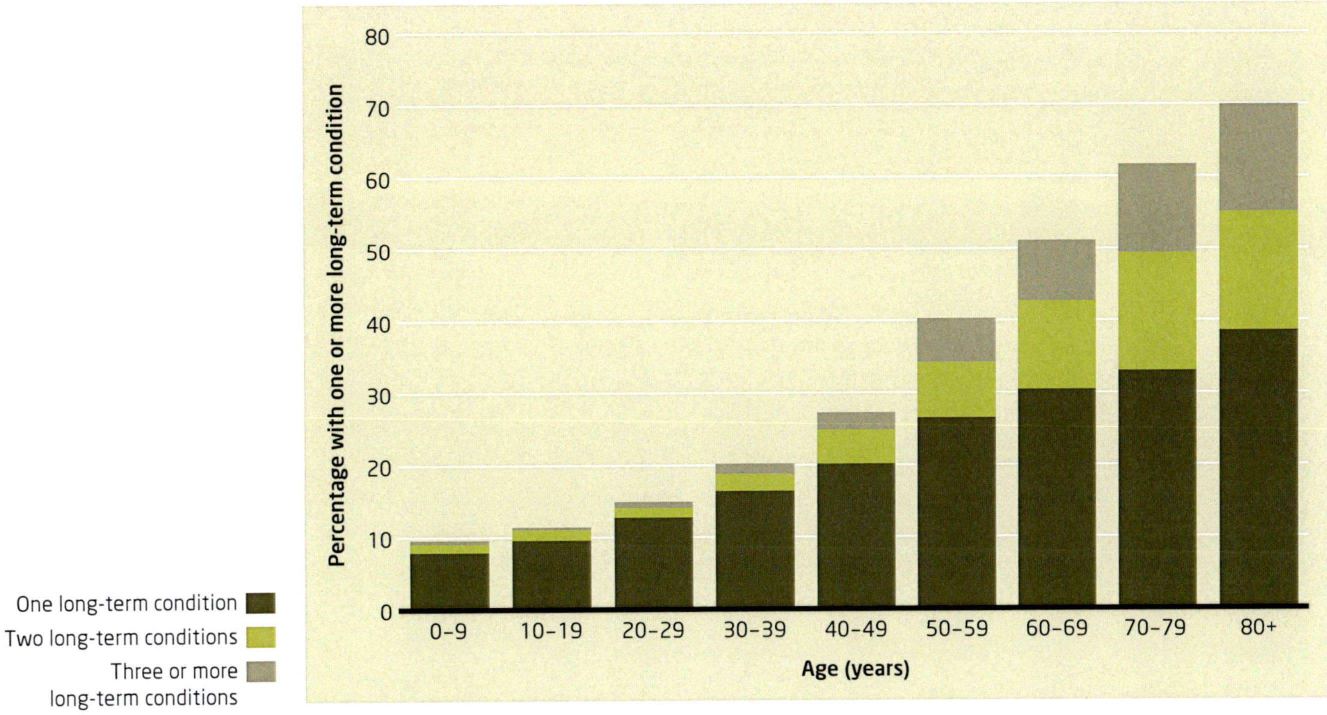

Source: Department of Health (2012a)

years of life people are living may not always be healthy years. In addition, increases in the prevalence of long-term conditions such as diabetes present many challenges to the health and social care system.

An estimated 15 million people in England have at least one long-term condition with the prevalence of cancers, chronic kidney disease and diabetes rising most quickly (Department of Health 2012a). The prevalence of long-term conditions increases with age, as shown in Figure 7, above. It is predicted that the number of people with long-term conditions will remain relatively stable over the next six years, although the number of people with multiple long-term conditions (known as multi-morbidity) is set to rise from 1.9 million in 2008 to 2.9 million in 2018 (Department of Health 2012a).

People with long-term conditions account for around 50 per cent of GP appointments, 64 per cent of outpatient appointments and 70 per cent of hospital bed days (Department of Health 2012a). Around 70 per cent of total health and care expenditure in England is attributed to people with long-term conditions (Department of Health 2012a).

People diagnosed with a number of long-term conditions are the most intensive users of health and social care services because their needs are usually more complex than those of people with single diseases. Most people aged 65 and over have multi-morbidity although a recent Scottish study found the absolute number of people with multi-morbidity was higher in those aged under 65, indicating its implications for the population as a whole (Barnett *et al* 2012). Multi-morbidity increases with deprivation. The likelihood of having a mental health problem increases as the number of physical morbidities a person has also increases.

According to one projection model, the number of people aged 65 and over in England with care needs, such as difficulty in washing and dressing, will grow from approximately 2.5 million in 2010 to 4.1 million in 2030, an increase of 61 per cent (Wittenberg *et al* 2011). Between 2010 and 2030, it is estimated that the number of younger adults with learning disabilities (aged 18–64) will rise by 32.2 per cent from around 220,000 to around 290,000, and the number of younger adults with physical or sensory impairment by 7.5 per cent from almost 2,900,000 to 3,100,000 (Snell *et al* 2011).

There are 700,000 people living with dementia in the United Kingdom (of whom approximately 570,000 live in England), and this figure is expected to reach 1.4 million over the next 30 years (Department of Health 2009). Among those with late-onset dementia, it has been estimated that 55 per cent have mild dementia, 32 per cent have moderate dementia and 13 per cent have severe dementia. The proportion considered to have severe dementia increases with age, reaching 23 per cent among people aged 95 and over (King's College London and London School of Economics and Political Science 2007). A high proportion of people with dementia need some care, ranging from support with activities of daily living, to full personal care and round-the-clock supervision.

The burden of disease has shifted away from life-threatening conditions to long-term conditions. Morbidity and disability caused by long-term conditions have increased, as have the numbers of older people with dementia. The needs of people with multi-morbidity present major challenges for the future.

Risk factors

Reductions in risk factors like cigarette smoking have contributed to falling rates of premature deaths from heart disease, strokes, cancers and respiratory diseases. At the same time new risk factors have emerged, most notably obesity and overweight, reflecting lifestyle and behavioural changes.

As illustrated in Figure 8, below, the proportion of adults in England with obesity has increased from 13 per cent of men and 16 per cent of women in 1993, to 26 per

Figure 8 Prevalence of obesity among people aged 16 and over, England, 1993–2010

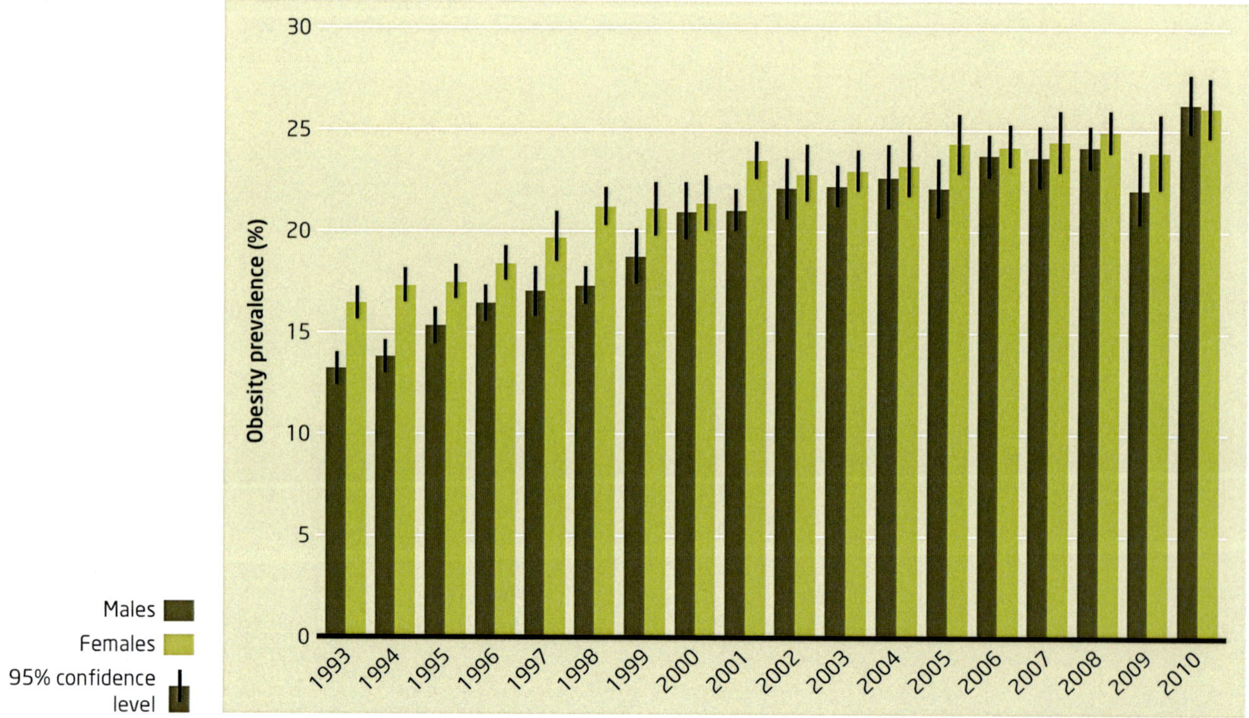

Source: National Obesity Observatory (2011)

cent of both men and women in 2010. The prevalence of obesity among children has also increased and is now 17 per cent among boys, and 15 per cent among girls (NHS Information Centre 2011a). Obesity rates in the United Kingdom are the highest in Europe (Organisation for Economic Co-operation and Development 2012).

It is estimated that by 2030 there will be 11 million more obese adults in the United Kingdom than in 2010, 3.3 million of whom will be aged 60 years or over (Wang *et al* 2011). If these trends are not reversed, there will be substantial increases in the number of people diagnosed with diabetes and other conditions associated with obesity, such as heart disease, cancer and arthritis. Rising obesity rates could also result in an expansion of morbidity in more disadvantaged communities and some minority ethnic groups.

Another important trend is the increasing number of alcohol-related deaths from liver disease, although this affects a much smaller proportion of the population. Alcoholic liver disease accounts for over a third (37 per cent) of liver disease deaths, and the number of deaths from liver disease in England rose from 9,231 in 2001 to 11,575 in 2009 (National End of Life Care Programme 2012). Average alcohol consumption has gradually fallen in many Organisation for Economic Co-operation and Development (OECD) countries over the past three decades, but has increased in the United Kingdom over the same period (Organisation for Economic Co-operation and Development 2011).

Risk factors such as obesity and alcohol misuse are not evenly distributed in the population. For example, there are three times as many deaths from alcoholic liver disease in the most deprived areas in England as in the least deprived (National End of Life Care Programme 2012). Deprivation also remains closely linked to obesity, with prevalence almost twice as high among children from the 10 per cent of most deprived local authority areas in England, compared to the least deprived 10 per cent (National Obesity Observatory 2011).

Smoking rates have fallen substantially but new risk factors have emerged. Alcohol consumption has risen and is responsible for increasing levels of alcohol-related morbidity and mortality. Obesity levels have also risen, and the consequences in terms of increased prevalence of diabetes and other conditions will be significant unless current trends are reversed.

Public and patient expectations

The long period of post-war economic growth benefited the baby boomers born in the 1940s; as a consequence, this generation has reached retirement with greater wealth and more generous pensions than at any time in history. It is of course from within this group that the most intensive users of health and social care services will be found in future. Some will also have sufficient resources to pay for health care in the private sector if they perceive that public services may not offer the quality of care they expect, or for social care if they do not qualify for support from the state.

The expectations of younger generations are often much higher and quite different from those of the post-war population that the NHS was originally set up to serve. These expectations reflect the transformation in standards of service in industries such as banking and retailing, and the revolution brought about through the use of technology and social media to engage with their customers. The NHS has been slow to keep up with these developments.

Choose and Book has given patients more control over hospital appointments, and the NHS Choices website now provides not only access to a wide range of information about health and health care, but also an opportunity for patients to comment on the services they receive. In addition, websites such as Patient Opinion and IWantGreatCare offer the public opportunities to learn about the experiences of others when making choices about which provider to use. Dr Foster has pioneered the development and use of information about the performance of services to support patient choice.

Although the Department of Health's information strategy for the NHS (Department of Health 2012b) sets out an ambitious vision for much greater online access by patients, including access to GP records from 2015, this is still very much the exception rather than the rule. Even simple changes in practice, such as email and telephone consultations with GPs and nurses, are not yet routine. With the exception of hospitals, most forms of health care are not easy to access outside of traditional working hours, meaning that the NHS is increasingly falling behind the standards set and experienced in other sectors.

Despite the majority of patients expressing a desire for shared decision-making, in 2006 nearly half of hospital patients in England said they were not sufficiently involved in decisions about their care (Coulter and Richards 2007). In social care, less than a third of users reported having as much control over their daily life as they wanted (NHS Information Centre 2011b). As well as involvement in decisions about the care they receive, patients have a key role to play in looking after their health and managing their health conditions, and yet health professionals do little to encourage patients in this role.

Patient and public expectations are rising. Increasingly, patients and service users expect health and social care services to be like other service industries and are willing to do more for themselves and interact with services via technology. They expect to be offered choice and variety and to experience services that are convenient, personalised and provided in modern buildings and healing environments.

Medical advances

Innovations in medical care, including new drugs, surgical procedures and diagnostic techniques, have contributed to improvements in both population health and the outcomes of care.

Conditions that were previously impossible to treat or that could be treated only with difficulty are now amenable to medical intervention. This means that lives can be saved (for example, in transplant surgery and neonatal care) and that quality of life can be improved (for example, through cataract surgery and hip replacements). Screening to detect diseases in their early stages is a good example of how medical advances support the prevention and not just the treatment of illness.

Medical advances have also enabled care to be delivered in different settings. In the case of mental health, advances in drug treatment and other interventions have revolutionised treatment, leading to a major shift away from the former psychiatric hospitals to much care now being provided in the community. Most of the care of people with learning disabilities has also moved out of hospitals into supported care in the community.

Advances in treatment have led to more care in acute hospitals being provided on an outpatient or day-case basis and to lengths of stay for inpatients being cut. The care of people who have had heart attacks is an example with a shift from several days of bed rest in hospital being superseded by the stabilisation and treatment of patients and their

Figure 9 Number of general and acute hospital beds, England, 1987/8–2009/10

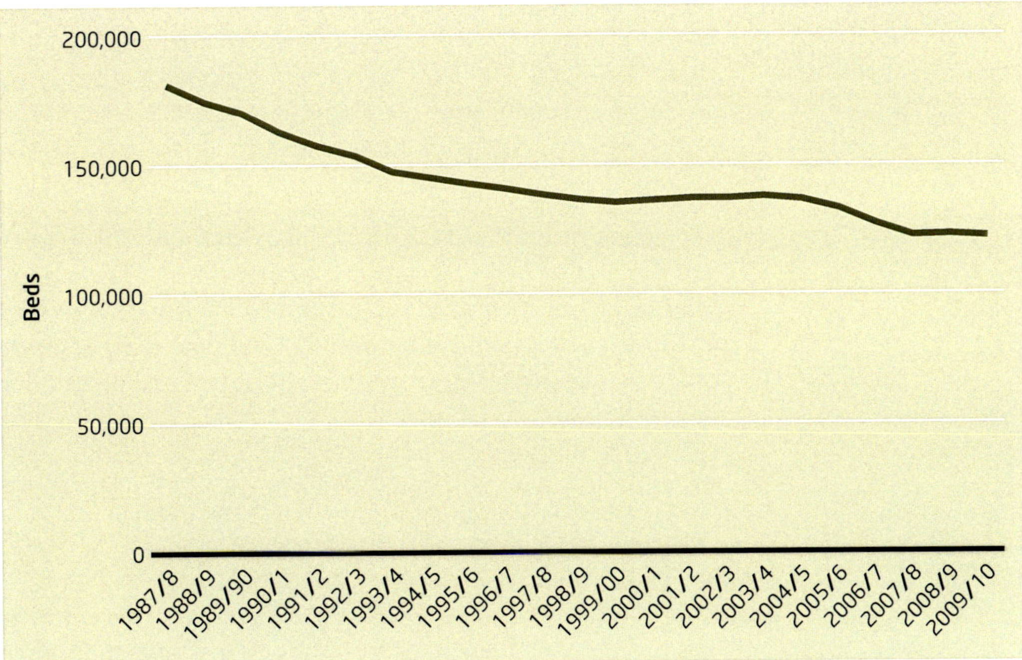

Source: Department of Health (2010)

early discharge. These changes have enabled the number of beds in acute hospitals to be reduced substantially, from 180,889 general and acute beds in 1987/88 to 121,756 in 2009/10, as shown in Figure 9, above.

Much routine management of people with long-term conditions is now done in GP surgeries instead of hospital outpatient departments, with nurses working alongside doctors to deliver care. Some practices are also offering a wider range of services through GPs with a special interest and by undertaking more diagnostic tests and minor surgery on their premises. Despite these developments, the essential features of general practice as a service provided by individual practices operating on a relatively small scale remain intact.

Likewise, the services provided by nurses, allied health professionals and social care staff in the community have changed at the margins and only recently have the opportunities to strengthen care out of hospital received serious attention. The under-development of community services may explain why policies to promote more care 'closer to home' have been slow to gain traction. We discuss below the important contribution of community health and social care services in developing new models of care.

Medical advances have resulted in an explosion of knowledge. This has created a challenge for health professionals in keeping up to date with evidence on how to treat patients with different conditions. In addition, patients now have much easier access to information through the internet, and this has started to change the relationship between patients and professionals.

Medical advances mean that those conditions that were previously impossible to treat are now amenable to medical intervention and that some diseases can be detected at an earlier stage. Technological advances have also enabled care to be provided in different settings, with more care being delivered on an outpatient or day-case basis and in general practice.

Financial and human resources

Public services in the United Kingdom face an unprecedented period of financial constraint as a consequence of the banking crisis that began in 2008 and its impact on the economy and public finances. The effects have been felt most strongly by local authorities, including social care, with the NHS relatively protected. The long-term macroeconomic outlook suggests that public spending will remain constrained for the foreseeable future.

Spending constraints on social care have led local authorities to tighten eligibility criteria, and this has resulted in an increase in unmet need. The proposals for reforming the funding of long-term care put forward by the Dilnot Commission were designed to establish a new settlement between the state and individuals. However, the cost of these proposals at a time of pressures on public spending has led the government to be cautious in its response (HM Government 2012). In the short term, additional funds are being transferred through the NHS to local authorities to help tackle the shortfall in social care spending, but it remains doubtful whether these funds will be sufficient.

In this context, national and local leaders will have to focus on ways of reducing waste and inefficiency. With acute hospitals having benefited most from recent increases in spending and the focus on investing in high-priority treatment services such as cancer and cardiovascular disease, improvements in care in the community are likely to depend on releasing resources from hospitals to invest in new services closer to home. This will present a major challenge at a time when many hospitals find themselves under pressure dealing with the demands being placed on them.

A high proportion of health and social care spending goes on human resources, with the number of staff working in the NHS increasing rapidly in recent years and pay also rising as result of new contracts agreed under the previous government. The age profile of the health care workforce means that a significant proportion will be retiring over the next 10–15 years, particularly health visitors and midwives. This could well lead to absolute shortages in the number of trained staff, but more likely, to a shortage of experienced senior staff to take on leadership and supervisory roles. In social care, while the workforce is older in comparison with the total working population of England, there is no evidence that it is getting older and, if anything, the range of ages is widening (Skills for Care 2010).

International migration of health professionals from the United Kingdom to the United States, New Zealand and Australia in particular has further increased the pressures on recruiting and retaining staff. If the relative pay gap internationally were to widen, there is a risk that the pull factors for trained health professionals to work overseas would increase. The question is whether this can be matched by inward migration.

A major challenge is aligning the skills of the workforce with the needs of patients. There is growing awareness that the current workforce is not well matched to patient needs, and the training pipeline, particularly of doctors, may exacerbate these problems. The Centre for Workforce Intelligence predicts that, by 2020, as the workforce ages, the NHS is likely to have an oversupply of hospital doctors but a shortfall in the number of GPs (Centre for Workforce Intelligence 2012).

A number of reports have emphasised the importance of using specialists and senior staff to deliver care for acutely ill patients, rather than relying so much on doctors in training (Thompson 2011; National Confidential Enquiry into Patient Outcome and Death 2007). The growing burden of chronic disease and multi-morbidity also demands a growth in generalist skills among doctors. Generalist skills are as important in hospitals as in primary care particularly in acute medicine where studies have shown the benefits of care provided in acute medical units staffed by generalists (Watcher and Bell 2012), as discussed later in the paper.

Public spending constraints mean that improvements in care will have to be funded out of existing budgets, and more intensive use made of existing assets. There is a need to use the workforce differently and to plan for how to deal with projected shortages and surpluses in key groups of staff. Despite an expansion in the medical workforce, there may be a shortage of GPs in future, while in hospitals there are opportunities to achieve a better balance between specialists and generalists.

Summary

Major progress has been made in tackling the principal causes of premature death in the post-war period and addressing risk factors like cigarette smoking. At the same time new challenges have emerged that pose a threat to population health in the future, most notably obesity and overweight. Health and social care services have played an important part in improving population health and providing access to care, and have evolved in response to changing needs.

Despite this, these services have struggled to keep pace with demographic changes, the shifting burden of disease and rising patient and public expectations. Too much care is still provided in hospitals and care homes, and treatment services continue to receive higher priority than prevention. Care is often fragmented, and the needs of an ageing population, among whom long-term conditions and multi-morbidity represent the greatest challenge, are not always well met.

2 How well equipped is the current delivery system to respond to the drivers of change?

The King's Fund's review of how far the NHS had come towards becoming a 'high-performing health system' following increased investments since 2001 and the reforms of the previous government concluded that major progress had been made in improving the performance of the NHS (Thorlby and Maybin 2010).

Notwithstanding this progress, there are no grounds for complacency. As we have shown, risk factors like obesity present challenges for the future; rates of cigarette smoking are still higher in England than in some other countries; health inequalities persist; and although survival rates for most cancers have improved, they remain lower than in many other countries. A particular area of concern is patient experience, where international comparisons show the United Kingdom not doing as well as many other countries (Davis *et al* 2010).

There is also room for improvement in social care where standards of provision are too variable and there are continuing concerns about the quality of care provided in people's homes and in residential settings. Recent reports into the care of older people have highlighted the challenge of providing health and social care with dignity and respect to vulnerable people. This includes ensuring effective co-ordination of care and integration between the many organisations and services concerned with the needs of older people who are today the main users of hospitals and care homes (Cornwell *et al* 2012).

If the health and social care delivery system is to rise to the growing challenges presented by long-term conditions and multi-morbidity, a fundamental and rapid reorientation is needed, with greater emphasis on integrated care and care delivered in settings other than hospitals and care homes.

We now go on to substantiate these arguments by analysing the shortcomings of the current models of care. This section of the paper is organised around a number of key themes:

- population health and health outcomes
- primary care
- hospital care
- social care
- mental health.

The aim is to summarise relevant facts and figures to demonstrate why fundamental change is overdue.

Population health and health outcomes

Analysis of health data from the Organisation for Economic Co-operation and Development (OECD), based on performance in 2009, show that the United Kingdom is in the 'middle of the pack' in terms of established indicators of health outcomes of the population. For example, the United Kingdom is slightly above the OECD average for potential years of life lost (PYLL) for women (2,479 PYLL per 100,000 compared with an average of 2,419) and slightly below for men (3,988 PYLL per 100,000 compared with an average of 4,689) (OECD 2011). Similarly, life expectancy rates for men and women in the United Kingdom are close to the OECD average (OECD 2011).

Comparing the United Kingdom with the best-performing OECD countries, there is clear scope for improvement in cancer survival rates and reducing deaths amenable to health care intervention. For example, survival rates in England for many cancers are improving, but not at the same rate as other countries. If England achieved survival rates at the European best, an additional 10,000 lives would be saved every year (Department of Health 2011a).

As shown in Figure 10, below, deaths amenable to health care interventions (such as selected childhood infections, treatable cancers, and complications of common surgical procedures) are relatively high in the United Kingdom (83 deaths per 100,000 in 2006/07, compared to 55 in France), notwithstanding progress in recent years.

Improving population health and health outcomes requires action to tackle the social and economic determinants of ill health and to bring about changes in lifestyle and behaviour. It also demands a much greater focus on prevention to enable smoking rates

Figure 10 Deaths amenable to health care interventions in 16 high-income countries, 1997/8 and 2006/7

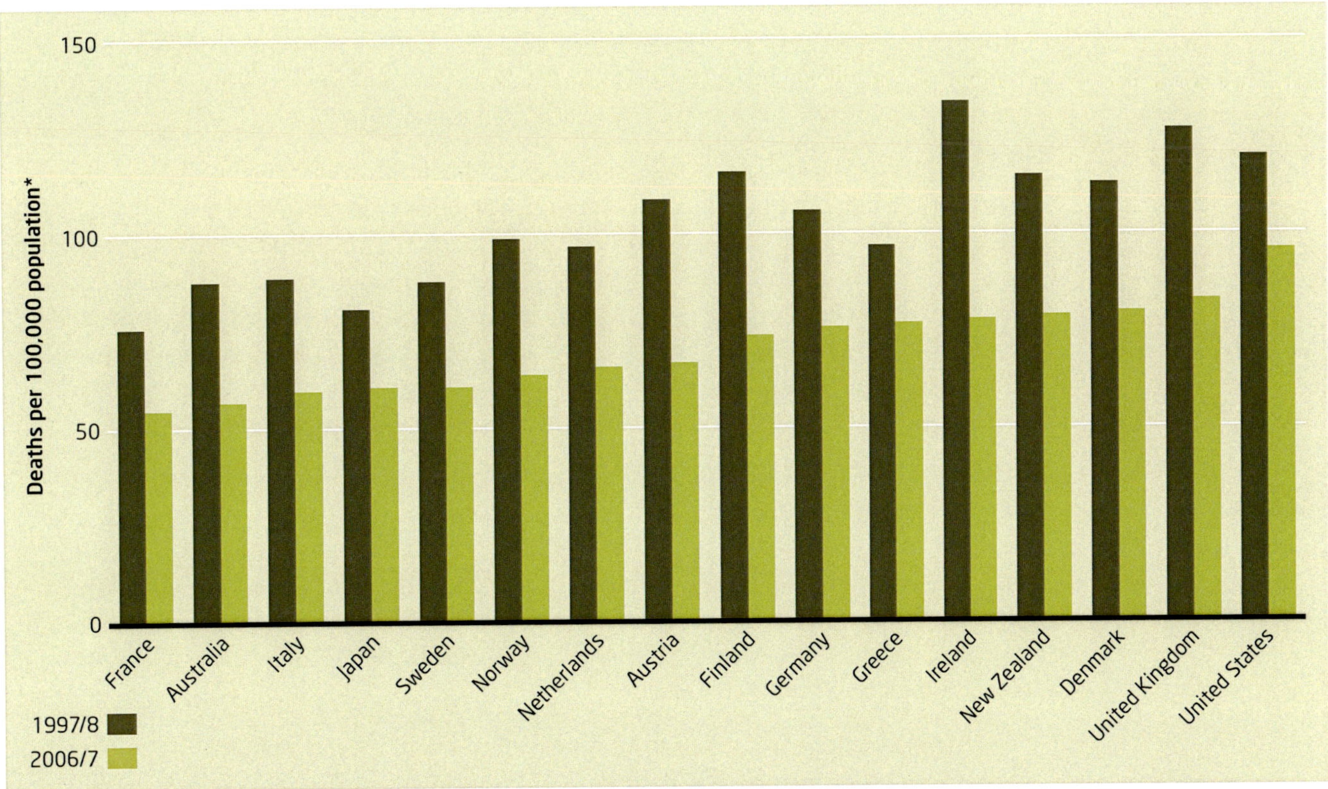

*Note: Countries' age-standardised death rates before age 75; including ischaemic heart disease, diabetes, stroke and bacterial infections. Analysis of World Health Organization mortality files and CDC mortality data for the United States.

Source: Adapted from Nolte and McKee (2011)

to be reduced to the levels found in the best-performing countries and to deal with other risk factors such as obesity and overweight. The NHS is still largely concerned with the treatment of illness rather than the promotion of health, and prevention remains the poor relation. For example, secondary prevention in primary care has received greater attention through the Quality and Outcomes Framework, but primary prevention is relatively neglected. There is the potential to do much more in primary care to support people to improve their health and to equip staff with the skills needed, for example, through staff training in motivational interviewing techniques. The 'Every Contact Counts' campaign recently announced by the government is another step in this direction.

The ageing population and changing disease burden mean that prevention is important at all ages, including among people aged 65 and over to ensure that further increases in life expectancy translate, as far as possible, into healthy years. Third-sector and community organisations are already playing a part in this, but their work is often poorly resourced and small scale. If the 'Big Society' is to be more than a slogan or sound bite, then public funding of third-sector organisations needs to be increased to support their work on a larger scale and on a sustainable basis.

Local government may be able to make a bigger contribution in future with the transfer of public health responsibilities from the NHS and the opportunity to work through transport, leisure, planning and education departments to improve population health. Health and wellbeing boards are well placed to provide leadership at a local level, and to develop strategies for health improvement that move beyond traditional silos to focus on communities and populations. Action across central government is also needed, for example, in relation to food-labelling and minimum pricing of alcohol.

Social care plays an important role in helping older people to remain independent, and yet the cuts in local government budgets have resulted in resources being increasingly focused on people whose needs are substantial or critical. This has made it more difficult to act early with relatively simple and inexpensive interventions that help people in their own homes. A recent study by the British Red Cross drew attention to the risk that a higher number of people will be admitted to hospitals and care homes as a result of the neglect of prevention in social care (British Red Cross 2012).

Health promotion initiatives need to recognise the limits of information-giving and harness insights from behavioural economics and other disciplines to understand how to change the behaviour of individuals and communities. This includes supporting people to make healthy choices, such as through the design of neighbourhoods that facilitate exercise, and using social networking and peer pressure in innovative ways, for example, to lose weight, stop smoking and take exercise. Change4Life is an example of a current programme that seeks to do this, but the emphasis needs to be on tackling multiple behaviours and risk factors rather than focusing on them separately.

The Marmot Review argued that action is needed across all the economic and social determinants of health, and should include giving every child the best start in life and strengthening the role and impact of ill health prevention (Marmot 2010). At present, services for families and children remain fragmented despite the creation of children's centres. There has been little concerted action to tackle the wider determinants of health at either national or local level, notwithstanding the use of health impact assessments and other public policy interventions.

In focusing on population health and prevention, there is a need to be mindful of the impact on health inequalities. Policies and actions that work for populations as a whole may inadvertently exacerbate health inequalities, unless they are tailored to the needs of different groups and address underlying causes.

Much greater priority needs to be given to public health and prevention in health and social care. While progress has been made in secondary prevention and improving life expectancy, health inequalities persist, and effective approaches to primary prevention and tackling the determinants of health are lacking. Services are still too heavily focused on treating ill health and dealing with acute need and those in crisis.

Primary care

Comparative studies have shown the United Kingdom in a positive light in the role of primary care and its contribution to improving population health and delivering value for money (Starfield 1998; Schoen *et al* 2009). A recent review of evidence from different sources concluded that the majority of care provided by general practice is of a good standard (The King's Fund 2011). Nevertheless, there is evidence of wide variations in the quality of care delivered, including the quality of diagnosis, and prescribing, referral and admission rates among patients with conditions that could be treated outside hospital (The King's Fund 2011).

There is also evidence that some practices vary in their ability to deliver care to patients with long-term conditions as recommended in guidance from the National Institute for Health and Clinical Excellence (NICE) (NHS RightCare 2011). A recent report from the National Audit Office (NAO) drew attention to the consequences of failing to provide care for people with diabetes in line with NICE standards (NAO 2012). According to the NAO, up to 24,000 people die each year from avoidable causes related to their diabetes, and the NHS could save an estimated £170 million through better understanding and management of people with this condition. While some of these savings would result from improving the quality of specialist care, some would also be made by reducing variations in the care delivered by primary care teams.

A specific concern has been late diagnosis and referral of patients with suspected cancer, which is related to the United Kingdom having lower survival rates than some other countries (Richards 2009). The more general point here is that 'There is significant scope for primary and community care providers to undertake more preventative activities that can lead to earlier diagnosis and treatment' (The King's Fund 2011). This observation is particularly important in view of the increased prevalence of long-term conditions and the opportunity to prevent some of these conditions through primary care.

There are wide variations too in admissions from a range of ambulatory care-sensitive conditions such as asthma, and evidence suggests that a proportion of these admissions could be avoided through more effective management in primary care (Purdy 2010; Dixon *et al* 2012). Evidence brought together in the NHS Atlas of Variation series documents the many opportunities to improve outcomes and release resources by reducing variations and providing care in line with evidence of best practice, including in primary care (NHS RightCare 2010, 2011).

This is illustrated in an analysis of children's services showing that death rates from illnesses that rely on first-access care, such as pneumonia and asthma, are higher in the United Kingdom than in Sweden, France, Italy, the Netherlands and Germany. The analysis found that if the United Kingdom performed to the same level as Sweden, then as many as 1,500 children a year might not die (Wolfe *et al* 2011). Lack of experience in paediatrics on the part of GPs and poor co-ordination of care with specialist teams in hospitals were identified as factors that helped to explain these differences.

Primary care also has scope to provide care that better meets the expectations of patients. Figure 11, overleaf, shows that in the lowest performing practices, only around a quarter

Figure 11 Percentage of patients able to see preferred doctor, England 2009/10

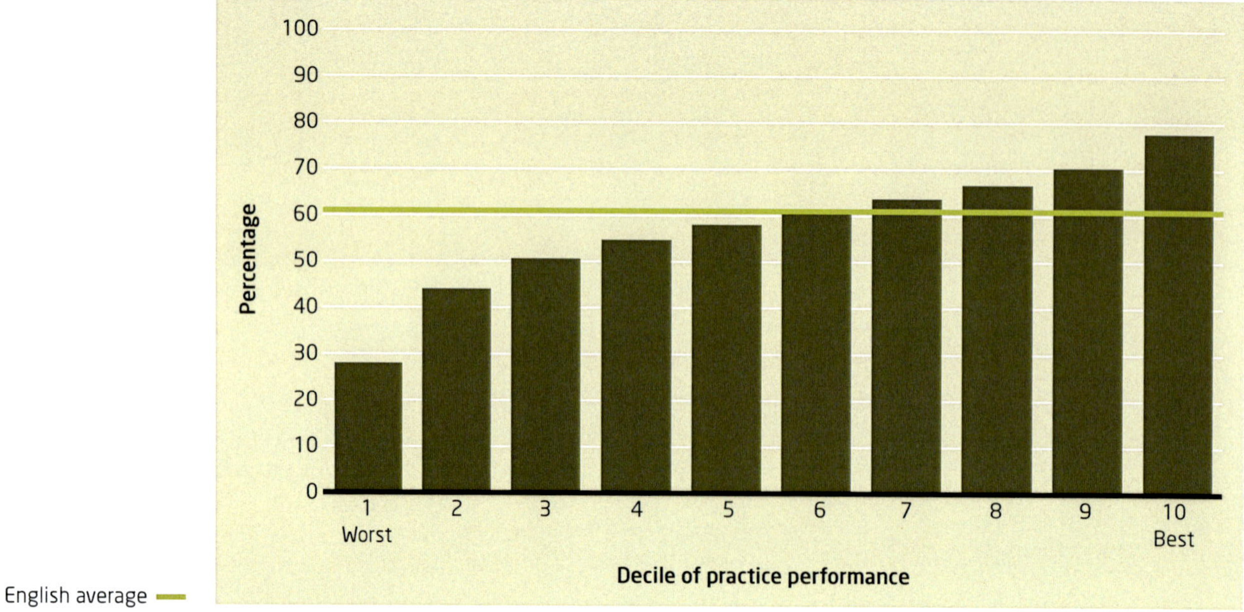

Source: GPPS (2009/10)

of patients report being able to see their preferred doctor. For patients with busy working lives it can be difficult to make an appointment at a convenient time, and there are concerns too about the quality of out-of-hours care. Also many practices have been slow to exploit opportunities to make greater use of the telephone and emails, in addition to face-to-face consultations.

Agreeing a care plan is important to empower patients with long-term conditions to make informed choices about their care, and yet evidence showed that in 2009/10 only 11 per cent of patients reported that they had been told that they had a care plan (The King's Fund 2011). There is also scope for practices to support patients to manage their conditions, for example, through monitoring their own blood pressure. Patient satisfaction with involvement in decisions about their care ranged from 53 per cent in the worst-performing practices to 84 per cent in the best-performing 10 per cent (The King's Fund 2011).

Poor-quality general practice is often concentrated in areas of greatest need, as Tudor-Hart observed when he coined the 'inverse care law' (Tudor-Hart 1971). Inequities in the distribution of GPs continue to exist, notwithstanding efforts to ensure that family doctors are available in relation to population need. For example, in 2009/10 there were almost two-fold variations in the ratio of GPs to the population served in England (The King's Fund 2011).

In many parts of the NHS, general practice still resembles a cottage industry in which family doctors as independent contractors run small businesses that are isolated from each other and constrained in the range of services they are able to provide. Alongside the lack of adequate premises and infrastructure, this means that it is difficult for practices to extend the scope of the services they deliver and the hours at which these services can be accessed. The current model of primary care also means that the work of practices is not well co-ordinated with that of specialist teams in hospitals and other expertise in the community, as in the example of children's services cited above.

In recognition of these challenges, the Royal College of General Practitioners (RCGP) – which has played a major part in raising standards in general practice – has argued that practices should work together in federations. In parallel, GPs in some parts of the country have taken the initiative to form larger practices in order to offer services such as specialist consultations, access to some diagnostic facilities and minor surgery, and minor-injury clinics. These developments have been supported by an investment in new buildings and equipment, through both the NHS and private sources.

Innovative practices are showing the way by delegating more tasks to nurses and other staff, enabling GPs to focus on diagnosis and urgent needs, and to lead the work of the primary care team. Larger practices are also able to make use of the specialist expertise of some GPs, thereby reducing the use of hospital services where clinically appropriate. The approach developed in Torbay and some other areas where a number of practices working in the same locality are aligned with an integrated health and social care team illustrates how community and primary care services can be co-ordinated more effectively around the needs of populations.

This approach is also important in indicating the scope for improving the performance of community services, which have been relatively neglected despite evidence of wide variations in practice and performance. If the inappropriate use of hospitals is to be reduced and care closer to home is to be enhanced, then much more attention needs to be given to the work of nurses and allied health professionals working in the community. It is crucial to develop strategies so that their work can be effectively integrated with that of primary care teams, and the services they provide can be made available 24/7 where appropriate. Social care needs to be part of these arrangements in view of the major role it plays in responding to the needs of older people and those with long-term conditions.

Although evidence on the cost-effectiveness of shifting services from hospitals to the community is inconclusive (Imison *et al* 2008; Munton *et al* 2011), there is increasing interest in finding ways of making better use of the skills of primary care teams and those of health and social care staff working in the community. This will require further investment in the buildings and infrastructure needed to make it happen, and the more rapid adoption of new ways of working (including communication and information technologies) already established in innovative practices. It will also require barriers between different services and professionals to be broken down to make a reality of integrated care.

Primary care in the United Kingdom is more firmly established than in many other countries and provides a wider range of care than at any time in the evolution of the NHS. Despite this, there is evidence of wide variations in the quality of care and inequities in the distribution of GPs. If the aim is to tackle these variations and to deliver more care out of hospital, the current cottage industry model of general practice is not fit for purpose.

Hospital care

Since the Hospital Plan of 1962, acute hospital care has been planned on the basis that every community should have access to the services of a district general hospital providing most forms of care other than highly specialised treatments. Advances in medicine and changes in the workforce mean that this is no longer possible. For example, there is increasing recognition that services such as emergency surgery may be unsafe out of hours, and the provision of these services needs to be concentrated in fewer centres that are better able to provide senior medical cover. Evidence from the NHS in London suggests that if the weekend mortality rate in London was the same as the weekday rate, there would be a minimum of 500 fewer deaths each year (NHS London 2011).

Changes in the location of care reflect evidence on the relationship between volumes of care and outcomes in some specialist services. Examples include vascular surgery, where the mortality rate is lower in high-volume hospitals than low-volume hospitals (Naylor R *et al* 2012), and paediatric heart surgery, where there are plans to cut the number of hospitals undertaking surgery to improve outcomes. There are also benefits from concentrating specialist stroke services in fewer hospitals, as has been shown in London, where an estimated 400 lives will be saved each year following the development of eight hyper-acute stroke units (Nicholson 2012).

Improving the quality of care often entails making available senior medical cover in some services on a 24/7 basis. This in turn means reducing the number of hospitals providing these services to enable consultant medical staff to operate effective rotas in the evenings and at weekends. Awareness of variations in outcomes is already forcing the pace of change in some areas, and further reconfigurations are certain to follow as district general hospitals limit their range of services and in some cases work as part of hospital networks.

The most contentious issues concern changes in the provision of accident and emergency and maternity services because of the importance attached to these services by patients and the public. Many of the changes being made derive from workforce shortages, for example, among consultants and midwives, making the current model of care unsustainable. This is leading to increasing differentiation in how these services are provided (eg, some hospitals providing midwife-led maternity care, and others no longer providing accident and emergency services at night).

Alongside these changes, there is a need to shift the location of care for older people who do not require specialist care in a hospital setting. As we have noted, older people make up the majority of patients in hospital beds, and yet many could be cared for elsewhere if appropriate facilities were available. The poor quality of care provided to older people in some hospitals is in part a reflection of the lack of adequate training for staff, as well as hospitals not being designed to meet older people's needs, and underlines the case for moving more care to alternative settings.

End-of-life care illustrates the inappropriate use of hospitals. Notwithstanding recent increases in the proportion of people dying at home, many still die in hospital, although they would prefer to be cared for in a hospice or their own homes. One of the challenges here is to make community services available 24/7 to stop hospitals becoming the default setting for lack of other options (Hughes-Hallett *et al* 2011).

Given the weight of evidence from different sources, there is an urgent need to improve the performance of services outside hospital and to bring about closer integration between hospitals and services provided in other settings. Investment in intermediate-care services that provide a rapid response to enable people to be cared for in their own homes, thereby avoiding admission to hospitals and care homes, is a key part of this. This applies particularly to the growing numbers of frail older people who often have complex mental as well as physical health needs and who account for a high proportion of bed use, as well as longer lengths of stay (Poteliakhoff and Thompson 2011; Cornwell *et al* 2012).

Fundamental changes in how acute hospitals work are essential. The quality of care provided in hospitals must be improved through further concentration of specialist services where this is supported by evidence, reduced duplication of local hospital services and more effective use of senior medical staff, including in the evenings and at weekends. There is an urgent need to care for frail older people and people at the end of life in alternative settings where appropriate.

Evidence from various sources has highlighted the following challenges in the current model of acute hospital care.

- Variations in performance between hospitals on indicators such as day surgery rates (National Audit Office 2010b; Appleby *et al* 2011) and lengths of stay for common causes of admission (Audit Commission 2003; Appleby *et al* 2010) illustrate the opportunity to reduce acute bed capacity.
- Opportunities exist to reduce emergency admissions to hospitals and emergency bed day use through early intervention in the community and more effective management in primary care of people with ambulatory care-sensitive conditions (Dixon *et al* 2012; Purdy 2010).
- A significant proportion of patients occupying beds do not need to be in hospital on clinical grounds (Goddard *et al* 2000; Audit Commission 2003), leading to problems in freeing up beds for patients who do need to be admitted.
- Many services provided in outpatient departments could be provided in other settings or may not need to be provided at all (eg, repeat outpatient appointments without clinical necessity) (Department of Health 2007; Imison *et al* 2008).
- The quality of care for some hospital patients is poor, especially older patients with complex needs for whom continuity of care in hospital is often lacking (Care Quality Commission 2011; Cornwell *et al* 2012; Local Government Association, NHS Confederation, Age UK 2012).
- Around one in 10 hospital admissions results in some form of harm, and between a third and a half of these events are thought to be preventable (House of Commons Health Committee 2009).

Social care

Nowhere is the need for fundamental change more apparent than in social care where arrangements rooted in the 1940s have not kept pace with the social and demographic changes described earlier in this paper. The King's Fund has argued that a more sustainable model of funding social care is required, and this should be based on a partnership funding model involving both public and private payers (Wanless 2006). However, reform of funding alone is not sufficient and should be accompanied by reform to the system of delivery, including a more integrated approach to the way social care and the NHS are commissioned and provided.

A major development over the past 30 years has been the increased role of the independent sector. There has been a progressive shift from care provided in the NHS, free at the point of use, to care becoming the responsibility of local authorities and subject to means-testing. In turn, many local authorities have outsourced their own services to external providers, and almost 90 per cent of social care services are now provided by private and third-sector organisations.

The implications of such a profound shift in the way care is commissioned and regulated have not always been thought through. The Law Commission's review of adult social care law has recommended radical reform of legislation and a single statute that would pave the way for a coherent social care system (Law Commission 2011). This would lead to a much clearer understanding of people's legal rights to care and support services, a new streamlined assessment and eligibility framework, and a duty on councils and the NHS to work together.

Rapid growth in the numbers of frail older people and younger people with disabilities has outstripped increased funding. A growing gap between needs and resources has led to a tighter rationing of care by local authorities, with 85 per cent restricting publicly funded care to those with substantial and/or critical needs (Association of Directors of Adult Social Services 2012). Social care resources are being directed towards high acuity and relatively expensive services, despite promising evidence of earlier interventions securing better outcomes in the long run (Humphries 2011).

The net result of these trends is that the publicly funded system is becoming more narrowly focused on those with the highest needs and lowest means. The numbers using these services are falling, with more people responsible for making their own private arrangements, often without adequate advice, information or support. In many parts of England, the private economy of care is already bigger than the publicly funded system, meaning that the default trajectory of the current system is towards one in which most people will be responsible for arranging and funding their own care in a private market.

There are concerns also about the quality of care that is offered both within residential care homes and in people's own homes. Regulation by the Care Quality Commission provides some safeguards against poor quality, but doubts remain about the ability of regulators to prevent well-publicised failures in the care of older people in residential settings, in part fuelled by concerns about a shift towards greater self-assessment by providers and fewer formal inspections. The risks of providers failing on business or financial grounds, as in the case of Southern Cross, highlight the absence of an effective market oversight or economic regulatory role.

Alternatives to residential care include extra care housing, sheltered housing and new forms of care in people's homes, many of which have been developed by the private and third sectors. However, there is limited choice for older people who want to move to specialist or alternative mainstream housing, in terms of tenure, location, size, affordability and type of care or support, and the specialist housing on offer does not always reflect older people's preferences (Pannell *et al* 2012). Over the next 20 years, it is estimated that the stock of specialist housing will need to grow by between 40 and 70 per cent (Pannell *et al* 2012).

The scope for technologies and innovations in care to enable people with complex needs to be cared for at home will be a major test for the health and social care system in future. The recent evaluation of the Whole System Demonstrator programme showed some benefits from telecare and telehealth (Steventon and Bardsley 2012), although not the transformation in care that advocates of these technologies hope for. Rapid changes in the available technologies and their cost may produce different results in future.

Another priority is to provide more personalised care through the greater use of direct payments and personal health budgets. Although not appropriate for everyone, evidence suggests that many do value the opportunity to make decisions about the care they need, rather than being offered a standard package of care determined by service providers (Davidson *et al* 2012). Service users and patients also expect care to be co-ordinated around their needs, including between health and social care. Nowhere is this more important than in the case of frail older people and people with complex needs. The separation between health and social care established in the post-war period is increasingly hampering the delivery of the seamless services that these people require as they move between different settings and their needs change. Areas of England that have found ways of overcoming this separation are reaping the benefits in terms of reduced use of acute hospitals and care homes (Thistlethwaite 2011).

The way in which social care services are delivered as well as funded needs radical overhaul. Personalisation, closer integration with health and housing and the use of technology create opportunities for innovation. New models of residential and home-based care are also needed, with a greater emphasis on people making informed choices about their care, however this is funded. Sufficient resources must be found through a combination of public and private sources to pay for care of the appropriate quality.

Mental health

Mental health services have gone through a radical transformation over the past 30 years – perhaps more so than any of the other service areas covered here. Deinstitutionalisation has seen the adoption of a dramatically different approach to care, with many other countries now looking to the United Kingdom as a pioneer in the development of community-based mental health services. The World Health Organization has highlighted England as one of the few countries in Europe with a comprehensive network of assertive outreach, early intervention and crisis resolution services (World Health Organization 2008). This is reflected in re-admission rates for schizophrenia and bipolar disorder, which are significantly lower in the United Kingdom than in most OECD countries (Organisation for Economic Co-operation and Development 2009).

It is important to acknowledge, however, that despite the transition to community-based care, inpatient services remain a core component of mental health care, and account for a significant proportion of overall mental health spending. Of the £6.5 billion spent on specialist mental health services for adults of working age, 40 per cent is accounted for by inpatient care in acute, secure or rehabilitation units (Mental Health Strategies 2011). Conversely, relatively little is spent on care for the very large numbers of people with less severe mental health problems who are supported mainly in primary care.

A recent analysis highlighted the gaps in treatment for people with depression and crippling anxiety conditions, with three-quarters of adults with these conditions, and three-quarters of children with problem behaviours, anxiety or depression, receiving no treatment (London School of Economics and Political Science 2012). The Improved Access to Psychological Therapies programme has sought to address this through a considerable expansion in the provision of NICE-approved psychological therapies. Nonetheless, the support available in primary care for people with mental health problems remains highly variable and limited in many areas, and long waiting times for treatment persist (Mind 2010).

A significant failing in the existing system is the separation of care for mental and physical illnesses, which is hard-wired into service provision, payment systems and professional training curricula. This institutional separation is at odds with the close relationship between mental and physical health, reflected in the high frequency with which illnesses of both kinds overlap in an age of multi-morbidity:

- approximately one in four patients in acute hospitals have dementia (Lakey 2009)
- around 30 per cent of patients with long-term physical conditions also have a mental health problem (Naylor C *et al* 2012)
- people with severe mental illnesses suffer from raised rates of physical illness, with a dramatic effect on life expectancy.

As a result of these inter-dependencies, inadequate treatment of mental health problems creates pressures both elsewhere in the NHS and for other public services. For example, it has been estimated that the extra costs of physical health care for people with mental health problems is at least £10 billion each year (London School of Economics and Political Science 2012), and between 12 and 18 per cent of all NHS expenditure on long-term conditions is linked to poor mental health and wellbeing (Naylor C *et al* 2012).

Rising rates of dementia represent a particular challenge to the system. Staff working in acute settings and GPs responsible for residents of care homes may not have adequate training in the care of people with dementia or delirium. Consequently, these conditions often go undiagnosed and are then inappropriately treated. The National Dementia Strategy stresses the need for improved detection, but this remains poorly implemented (National Audit Office 2010a).

Despite considerable investment in community-based mental health care, the wider social outcomes experienced by people with mental health problems remain poor. Many experience significant challenges related to employment, housing and welfare, and find that the services delivered to support them with these issues are poorly integrated. Recent policy documents have emphasised the importance of social inclusion and stressed that mental health services should aim to support people's recovery in a broad sense, beyond narrow clinical objectives.

Although mental health care in England fares well in many international comparisons, the current model of care is still failing in a number of respects. The system treats mental health problems in isolation from physical needs and misses opportunities to connect with other public services that are essential to recovery. Overcoming these weaknesses could relieve pressure in other parts of the system, where physical illnesses are exacerbated by unresolved mental health problems.

Summary

The health and social care system gives too little priority to preventing illness and actively supporting people to live independent and healthy lives. The cottage industry model of general practice is not fit for purpose if the aim is to reduce variations in care and deliver more care out of hospital, where appropriate. Major changes in how acute hospitals work are essential to tackle variations in quality and patient safety.

There is an urgent need to provide more care in alternative settings where appropriate, such as at the end of life, and there are opportunities for some work currently done in hospitals (eg, certain diagnostic tests and some outpatient appointments) to be provided in the community. The funding and provision of social care are in need of radical overhaul. New models of residential care are required to enable people to live independently for as long as possible.

While we have highlighted shortcomings in each of the main sectors of the health and social care system, it is often the failure of these different elements to work together that is of greatest concern to patients and users. The traditional dividing lines between GPs and hospital-based specialists, hospital and community-based services, and mental and physical health services mean that care is often fragmented and poorly co-ordinated. Despite growing recognition of the benefits of holistic, patient-centred, team-based care and of generalism, as well as specialist knowledge, integrated care is the exception rather than the rule.

Our analysis leads us to conclude that patching up the existing system will not deliver the transformational changes required. Nothing less than a sea change in thinking and action is needed to tackle the fundamental weaknesses of a system that remains focused on addressing yesterday's problems rather than anticipating what will be needed in future. In making these points we reiterate that the NHS is not alone in the need to fundamentally reorient how care is delivered, as other systems around the world have been just as slow to adapt to changing needs.

3 The health and social care system of the future

'If I had asked people what they wanted, they would have said a faster horse.'

Attributed to Henry Ford

In this section we go beyond a critique of existing arrangements to outline a number of cross-cutting changes to the health and social care delivery system that we believe hold potential for enhancing quality, reducing costs and making the system fit for the future. We describe areas of innovation that challenge assumptions about existing models of care and signal promising areas of development. In subsequent work, we will further examine this potential, we will ask whether these areas of innovation can achieve the necessary step-change in the delivery of care, and we will assess the extent to which there is evidence to support their effectiveness.

This section will explore the following in turn:

- enhancing the role of patients and users in the care team
- changing professional roles
- rethinking the location of care
- using new information and communication technologies
- harnessing the potential of new medical technologies
- making intelligent use of data and information.

In discussing the opportunities offered by innovations in care in these areas, it is worth remembering an observation attributed to William Gibson to the effect that 'The future is already here – it's just not very evenly distributed'. Acting on this insight, we draw on examples of organisations and technologies that illustrate where and how care is already being delivered differently, and the changes in practice that are occurring as a consequence. These examples contain important clues on how the health and social care delivery system might look in future, although further analysis is needed to understand whether the system can deliver the anticipated benefits in practice.

Enhancing the role of patients and users in the care team

Over the past two decades consumers have become increasingly involved in the design and creation of products and services. Through co-designing with customers, industries and services have sought to better meet the needs of end-users. The principle of co-design is now beginning to be applied to health care, with patients working in partnership with professionals to design services and care pathways. This is helping to generate innovative ideas, resulting in positive changes for both users and staff (The King's Fund 2012a).

The concept of co-production has also been applied to health and social care, with patients and service users being supported to share decision-making, and to self-manage their health and care. The approach draws on the skills, knowledge, time and expertise of service users, and regards the relationship between clinicians and patients as a meeting of two experts, challenging the perception of service users as passive recipients of care. Co-production has been described as requiring professionals to move from being 'fixers to facilitators', with a redistribution of power towards service users (Realpe and Wallace 2010).

It is important to recognise that patients and service users have very different motivations and capacities to play a bigger part in the design and delivery of care. There have been a number of attempts to capture this by segmenting patients according to different dimensions. For example, the Department of Health developed a model that divides patients into: 'fighters', 'thrivers', 'disengaged' and 'survivors' (Department of Health 2008). Patients with chronic conditions also vary in their skills, knowledge and confidence to self-manage their conditions, and support must be tailored to individuals and their circumstances.

Evidence shows that there are wide gaps between what patients want and what doctors think that patients want. When patients are fully informed about the risks and benefits of treatment options, they choose different and often fewer treatments. Mulley and colleagues make a convincing case for doctors to have more and better information about what patients truly want, and for patients to have more and better information about options, outcomes and evidence (Mulley *et al* 2012). They argue that systematic measurement and reporting of patient preferences is essential to avoid the 'silent misdiagnosis'.

Decision-support aids can help to enable shared decision-making, as can coaching patients before consultations and giving them lists of questions to ask their health professional. Through the MAGIC programme (Making Good Decisions in Collaboration), The Health Foundation is working with frontline professionals to test different ways of encouraging shared decision-making across a number of sites – for example, where women with early-stage breast cancer are supported to choose between mastectomy and breast-conserving surgery. Learning so far demonstrates the importance of clinical teams not only understanding the concept of shared decision-making, but also having the skills to put shared decision-making into practice (The Health Foundation 2012).

Self-care has been shown to enable people with long-term conditions to take control of their health, and to enhance independence and quality of life. The Year of Care programme set out to deliver personalised care for people with long-term conditions in routine practice, using diabetes as an exemplar (NHS Diabetes 2012). Through care planning, patients were actively involved in deciding, agreeing and owning how their diabetes would be managed, working in partnership with a health care professional. People with diabetes reported improved experience of care and real changes in self-care behaviour (Diabetes UK, Department of Health, The Health Foundation, NHS Diabetes 2011).

Self-directed care is complementary to self-care and involves patients and service users being allocated a budget with which they can decide on the services and support they need. Originally developed in social care through direct payments, self-directed care has been extended to health care through individual budgets and personal health budgets. Although not appropriate for all users and patients, as discussed earlier self-directed care has been shown to deliver benefits especially in delivering care that is more personalised and customised to the needs of individuals (Davidson *et al* 2012).

Involving lay workers in promoting health and delivering services is another approach that shows promise. A number of NHS organisations are now engaging peer support workers to provide support for people with mental health problems, and there is evidence that this can reduce the likelihood of psychiatric hospitalisation and demand for other services (Naylor and Bell 2010). A different example is the work carried out in Northumbria Healthcare NHS Foundation Trust to introduce a stroke volunteer support programme, whereby people with personal experience of stroke provide psychosocial information and support for stroke patients and carers during their hospital stay. The programme has been found to reduce anxiety and isolation and increase confidence, and provides practical coping strategies and positive role models (Coulter 2012).

Outside the United Kingdom there are examples of health services that have already made radical shifts to put care in the hands of patients. For example, renal patients at the Ryhov County Hospital in Jönköping, Sweden, receive training to use dialysis machines, read and interpret laboratory results, and document their care, and are also able to use exercise machines and equipment while receiving dialysis. This patient-inspired model has resulted in more frequent dialysis among patients who find the process less burdensome, leading to reduced infection rates and complications. Nearly 60 per cent of peritoneal dialysis and haemodialysis patients in the clinic are now managing their own treatments in this way (Institute for Healthcare Improvement 2012).

There is a growing emphasis on asset-based approaches to promoting health and wellbeing in marginalised communities that utilise the capacity, skills, knowledge, connections and potential within the community, rather than focusing on the needs and problems (Improvement and Development Agency 2010). There is some evidence that lay community health champions can be effective and cost-effective in changing behaviour, although formal evaluations are required (South *et al* 2010; Woodall *et al* 2012). 'Altogether Better', a programme hosted by NHS Yorkshire and Humber, has so far trained over 15,000 volunteer community and workplace health champions to signpost people in their families, communities and workplaces to services, and to motivate involvement in healthy social activities and groups (Altogether Better 2008–12).

The health and social care system will be fit for the future when patients and users are actively involved in designing care, are seen as key members of the care team and are given adequate support and information to enable them to self-care and manage their condition.

Changing professional roles

Self-care has potential not only to improve patient outcomes and experience, but also to reduce the burden on health and social care professionals and make the most appropriate use of their skills. With much of the health and social care budget spent on staff, exploring ways of using the workforce differently is likely to assume increasing importance. Changes to professional roles inevitably challenge entrenched interests and may require alterations to the regulation of care if the productivity challenge is to be met and workforce constraints addressed.

It is increasingly recognised that care outcomes are a function of a team's performance, rather than the knowledge, skills and competencies of individual professionals. The health and social care system of the future will require staff who are team players and who are able to adapt their skills to changing patient needs. This will enable care to be provided by staff who have the most appropriate skills, allowing the most senior and qualified staff to perform only those functions that cannot be better undertaken by others. Changes to the education and training of health and social care professionals, including closer integration of training, are needed to facilitate team working.

There are many examples of staff being used differently to support moves in this direction. In maternity services, for example, there is some evidence that midwives can effectively perform tasks that are usually performed by doctors without compromising safety or quality of care (Sandall *et al* 2011). Available evidence suggests that nurses working as substitutes or supplements for doctors in defined areas of care can provide the same quality of care and similar outcomes, and that patients are equally or more satisfied (Laurant *et al* 2010). However, there is also some evidence that more resources are used in nurse-led than physician-led care, for example, through nurses ordering a higher number of tests and investigations (Laurant *et al* 2010).

In some areas of care, allied health professionals are substituting for or supplementing doctors. This includes physiotherapists triaging orthopaedic outpatients; pre-hospital thrombolysis being undertaken by ambulance paramedics trained as emergency care practitioners; and radiographers screening, conducting examinations, and interpreting X-rays in place of radiologists (Laurant *et al* 2010). A different example is the use of care co-ordinators with no formal professional training to support nurses, allied health professionals and social care professionals working in integrated community health and social care teams (Thistlethwaite 2011).

Some of the most innovative examples of changing professional roles are found in the emerging economies of the world. The Aravind Eye Care System in India delivers care in rural areas of Tamil Nadu and employs paramedics to perform a wide range of largely repetitive clinical activities, with a ratio of ophthalmologists to paramedics of 1:5. Tasks performed by paramedics include outpatient examinations (eg, taking preliminary history, recording vitals, and checking the intra ocular pressure) and patient counselling for surgery. The approach aims to allow doctors to focus on areas where they are uniquely equipped to make a difference.

The emphasis on team care and the use of a wide range of skills in part reflects advances in medicine that have shifted many forms of care from problem-solving mode towards a rule-based regime. Under this regime, the focus is on applying evidence-based protocols and practices as effectively and systematically as possible. In many cases this entails using less-experienced caregivers in place of those who are more experienced, as in the examples we have cited. This in turn frees up doctors and other skilled professionals to use their skills to diagnose and treat conditions where there is greater uncertainty (Christensen *et al* 2000).

Making effective use of the workforce in the NHS also means ensuring the right mix of generalists and specialists. In hospitals, for example, there is evidence to support the growing use of general acute physicians to co-ordinate the care of acutely ill patients during the first few days of admission. Acute medical units are associated with lower inpatient mortality, improved patient and staff satisfaction, reduced hospital stays and increased throughput (Watcher and Bell 2012). There are similarities with the role of hospitalists in the United States but, unlike acute physicians in the NHS, hospitalists co-ordinate care *throughout* a patient's hospital stay.

There is also evidence of the need for greater use of specialists in some areas of care and for greater continuity of care by specialists. For example, as mentioned earlier, there is a correlation between hospital mortality and the number of senior doctors working in hospitals at weekends (Dr Foster 2011; NHS London 2011). There is also evidence of the benefits of continued consultant cover in acute medical units. This has led the Royal College of Physicians (RCP) to argue that these units should be staffed by specialists who are present for more than four hours for seven days a week in order to reduce mortality rates and emergency re-admissions among acutely ill patients (Royal College of Physicians 2012).

The health and social care system will be fit for the future when we have more flexible professional roles that allow care to adapt to the changing needs of patients. This includes all team members being clear about their roles and responsibilities, and being empowered to undertake as many responsibilities as they are able (including patients and lay workers). The system also needs to ensure an appropriate mix of generalists and specialists.

Rethinking the location of care

Any fundamental re-think of the health and social care system must include consideration of where care is best provided, the facilities that are needed and how assets can be used most effectively. This has major implications both for the role of acute hospitals and where patients access services. There are many opportunities to move more care out of hospitals and into the community, including the provision of step-down care and rehabilitation closer to home. There are also opportunities to achieve much closer integration between different providers of care both within the NHS and between health and social care.

The potential to make fundamental changes in the location of care and to achieve closer integration is well illustrated by the reform of the US Veterans' Health Administration (VA) in the 1990s. Under the leadership of Ken Kizer, the VA was transformed from a fragmented hospital-centred system to an organisation based on a series of integrated service networks serving each VA region. This resulted in a 55 per cent reduction in the use of hospital beds and a measurable improvement in the quality of care (Kizer 2001). These changes were achieved by investing in a range of services outside hospitals and were facilitated by the use of telehealth and telecare technologies.

In the system of the future, the vision should be of 'home as the hub' of care, enabling patients and service users to take greater responsibility for their health and wellbeing, with the support of carers and families. Innovative providers are already demonstrating the scope for providing services in people's homes that may previously have been available only in hospitals. This includes, for example, the provision of intravenous antibiotics, chemotherapy for cancer patients and home haemodialysis for renal patients. Home care may also include the delivery of medication for patients with conditions such as rheumatoid arthritis and multiple sclerosis, and continuing health care for patients (including children) with complex needs (Taylor 2012).

There is an urgent need for housing provision to support healthy ageing and promote independence through homes that are well designed, appropriately located and energy-efficient. Early support through aids and adaptations, handyperson schemes and telecare will be fundamental. The level and intensity of care and support should adjust flexibly to meet needs arising from frailty, dementia or other forms of ill health so that people can remain in their own home for as long as possible, this being the overwhelming preference of older people.

For some older people, moving house, especially to housing with access to care, improves quality of life, physical health and social wellbeing (Pannell *et al* 2012). Extra care housing, for example, is designed to meet both the current and future needs of residents and offers access to care and support 24-hours a day on site and on call. It can therefore be a home for life, as well as a viable alternative to residential care for frail older people who need more intensive support. Evidence shows that extra care housing can improve health and wellbeing, and provides the economies of scale for delivering cost-effective care and support (Housing Learning and Improvement Network and Association of Directors of Adult Social Services 2011; Netten *et al* 2011).

Primary care has huge potential to support the relocation of care and the delivery of services closer to home. Access to community diagnostics could be facilitated if general practices were able to operate these on a shared basis through federations, super partnerships or networks alongside specialists, where appropriate. If there is to be a radical relocation of care, then GPs, specialists, nurses and other clinicians will need to be supported to work in 'teams without walls' (Royal College of Physicians, Royal College of General Practitioners, Royal College of Paediatrics and Child Health 2008). This model is particularly relevant to medical (as opposed to surgical) specialties such as diabetes and rheumatology, as well as paediatrics and the care of older people with complex needs.

In future, acute hospitals will be used for people who need care that cannot be provided more appropriately or effectively in other settings. The shape of things to come is illustrated by initiatives such as the Right Care Right Here programme to redevelop hospital services in west Birmingham, where two acute hospitals will be replaced by a new acute facility, with a planned 35 per cent reduction in acute beds. The programme entails investing in services outside the hospital to enable the new, smaller hospital to deal with the demands placed on it by working closely with other providers of health and social care. The new model also involves the majority of outpatients, diagnostics and surgical day-case activity being shifted from acute hospital departments to community facilities. There will also be increased community-based urgent care and out-of-hours services as alternatives to accident and emergency (A&E). Enhanced intermediate-care provision will support rehabilitation and recovery close to home through both beds and new community-based teams. A key component of the model will be new services in primary care health centres that support healthy lifestyles (Sandwell and West Birmingham Hospitals Trust 2009).

In future, some services that are currently delivered in district general hospitals will move to specialist centres, where the evidence shows that this will deliver better outcomes. A strong argument can be made for hospitals in future to work increasingly as part of networks to provide the public with access to the right care in the right place. These networks will link district general hospitals with each other and with specialist hospitals to enable care to be provided locally where it can and in specialist centres where appropriate. The development of cancer and cardiac networks, and the establishment of academic health sciences centres and networks in some areas, foreshadow this way of working.

There are also opportunities to 're-invent' hospitals by separating their role in treating patients whose needs really are acute from their role in caring for and rehabilitating patients who cannot yet be safely discharged home or supported in the community. Both functions could continue to be performed in hospitals (not least because of the long-term investments made in modernising hospital facilities), but could be managed separately to signal the distinctive needs of the patients concerned and the care they require. This might enable concerns about the care and dignity of older people in hospitals to be addressed more effectively.

There are some similarities between this approach and 'patient hotels', which provide accommodation for patients who do not require intensive hospital-based care but who need to remain within the hospital campus, such as cancer patients receiving daily treatment, and patients staying before or after an operation. The patient hotel concept, which started in Sweden, is now being adapted by a number of NHS hospitals. Great Ormond Street Hospital for Children NHS Foundation Trust, for example, offers short-term accommodation for day-care patients who do not need the acute services of an inpatient ward and for their families.

Across the public sector there are opportunities to better organise the community estate and to create one-stop facilities for housing, benefits, health care and other services. Co-location can be more convenient for users, and while not sufficient on its own to engender better co-ordination between health, social care and other services, it does have the potential to help enable more integrated and timely care (Imison *et al* 2008). There is also scope to deliver care in more convenient settings, for example, by high-street pharmacies providing a wider range of services, and GP surgeries or nurse-led clinics being located in supermarkets.

The health and social care system will be fit for the future when as much care as can be provided safely and efficiently is delivered at or near people's home, when assets are utilised to their full extent and are flexible to adapt to changing usage, and when community-based facilities promote integrated working and provide convenient access for users.

Using new information and communication technologies

Information and communication technologies have the potential to revolutionise patients' and users' experience, transforming both how and where care is delivered, as can be seen in other sectors. That it is now possible to scan a barcode on your phone, add the product to an online shopping basket, place the order and arrange delivery may seem strange to those for whom shopping has traditionally meant travelling to a supermarket, taking products off the shelf, checking them out with a cashier, and then transporting them home. By comparison, the experience of seeing a doctor or having a blood test has changed little as a result of such technologies.

Mobile phone apps already provide lifestyle and health advice, such as the NHS Direct symptom checker, and the Met Office *Healthy Outlook* service, which provides recorded voice calls for chronic obstructive pulmonary disease (COPD) patients when environmental conditions are forecast that would exacerbate their health. There are also NHS clinics for sexually transmitted infections that now send test results by text message. In future, the use of smart phones in health care could include personalised exercise or dietary plans, motivational messages and alerts, and could assist people in locating the nearest health facilities. Other apps can enable the capture of data on activities and vital signs, and the transmission of data to health and social care professionals (CSC Leading Edge Forum 2010).

Patients are increasingly going online for health information and advice, to self-diagnose and to post comments about their experience of care in hospital or from GP practices. This will become even more common in the future as access to the internet becomes ubiquitous through wireless technologies and increased use of mobile devices. In 2010, among those who had used the internet in the past three months, 39 per cent overall, and 44 per cent of those aged 55–64, had used it to seek health-related information (Office for National Statistics 2011g). The next cohort of older people will be much more comfortable using the internet to manage their health and engage with health and social care professionals. The Department of Health's recent information strategy describes how in future patients will be able to routinely access their health records online, interact with professionals electronically, and ultimately share care plans, preferences and support needs with everyone who provides their care (Department of Health 2012b).

Electronic health communication interventions can help promote self-management and shared decision-making, and provide direct access to peer and expert support.

The Comprehensive Health Enhancement Support System (CHESS), developed by the University of Wisconsin, provides information and interactive coaching tools, and enables patients and carers to communicate with their clinical team, as well as with other patients and their own social support networks. CHESS has been used by people with cancer and heart disease (including heart patients in the United Kingdom), and is being adapted and trialled to support other groups such as older people and people with alcohol dependence (Center for Health Enhancement Systems Studies 2012).

Other health care systems have already harnessed new information and communication technologies to transform how they provide care. Kaiser Permanente, for example, uses a comprehensive health information system – KP HealthConnect – that includes a secure patient portal, allowing patients to view portions of their record, access test results, email providers, order repeat prescriptions and arrange appointments. In 2009, as many as 3.3 million patients had obtained user IDs and passwords to access the secure features of KP HealthConnect (Liang 2010). In the same year an average of 361,000 members were sending a total of 700,000 e-messages to their providers each month (Christensen and Silvestre 2010). There is emerging evidence that the 'email your doctor' function has contributed to changes in the ways in which patients access services. Hawaii was the first region to implement the KP HealthConnect system in an outpatient setting in 2004, and a study found a reduction in visits per patient of 26 per cent between 2004 and 2007, as patients made greater use of scheduled telephone consultations and secure messaging (Chen *et al* 2009).

Group Health Cooperative in Seattle, Washington, is another health care system that has experienced changes in how patients access care through the use of technology. Like KP HealthConnect, Group Health Cooperative was an early adopter of the electronic patient care record, and many more contacts between patients and doctors today take place by telephone and email. This has enabled face-to-face consultations to be extended in length and to be used primarily for patients with more complex needs that cannot be met in other ways. A family physician in Group Health Cooperative may see 12 or 13 patients in a typical working day with each appointment lasting for an average of 30 minutes. The use of technologies is supported by changes in professional roles with nurses and other members of the team working closely with family physicians.

New information and communication technologies can also support clinicians to deliver safe and high-quality care for patients remotely. It is now possible to live-stream patients' data, such as pathology or radiology results, to a smart phone, allowing clinicians to interpret and respond to information from a remote location or in another part of the hospital. There are also technologies that enable remote intensivists to continually observe patients in multiple intensive care units from a single remote location, making it possible for hospitals to deliver intensive care without trained intensivists on site. Patient information can be provided to remote intensivists through audio and video monitoring and through direct connection to physiological monitoring systems (that provide automatic alerts to problems) and other information systems in hospitals, such as pathology and radiology.

The health and social care system will be fit for the future when patients and users are able to interact with providers at a time and place convenient to them, using available technologies, and are supported to be cared for at home using telehealth and telecare.

Harnessing the potential of new medical technologies

Advances in medical science and technologies are also likely to have a significant impact on future models of care but in ways and timescales that are difficult to predict. In some areas such as personalised medicine, they are also likely to raise regulatory and ethical challenges (Mirnezami *et al* 2012).

There are a number of potential opportunities.

- The miniaturisation and automation of drug delivery resulting in improved drug compliance and safety, and allowing more care to be delivered in a home or community setting, overseen by non-medical staff or indeed self-administered by the patient or family member.
- 'Precision' or personalised medicine, whereby molecular profiling can be used to determine diagnostic, prognostic and therapeutic strategies that are precisely tailored to an individual's requirements. For example, analysing biopsy tissue for genetic variants can predict whether a cancer will respond to a specific treatment.
- Genomic profiling replacing genetic testing, resulting in more detailed information about a person's predisposition to disease and more proactive prevention.
- Further refinement of existing drug regimens and treatments, combined with new technologies for delivery, enabling more targeted treatments (both for population sub-groups, and for the affected part of the body), thus increasing efficacy and reducing side-effects.
- Smaller sensors for high-definition monitoring, which can be worn by the patient while remaining mobile.
- The next generation of compact, light and less costly robotic systems and miniature robots (so called 'virtual surgical simulation tools'), enabling procedures and transplants to be conducted more efficiently and potentially in non-hospital settings.
- Prostheses for amputees that can be controlled directly through electrodes implanted into the brain, enabling much greater levels of functioning for people with physical disabilities.
- Regenerative therapies using stem cells, or reprogramming adult cells, although the potential for effective and safe regenerative therapies beyond bone marrow transplants remains elusive and expensive, despite 50 years of medical trials.
- Increased miniaturisation of equipment, enabling community staff to support patients and service users through technologies previously available only in hospitals.

In the past, advances in medical science and technologies have tended to increase overall expenditure – the key challenge for the future will be for these to improve health, while also reducing the overall cost of services. The National Institute for Health and Clinical Excellence (NICE) has a key role to play here. Historically, the spread of inventions within the NHS has often been slow, and it will be important to ensure that the adoption and diffusion of cost-effective technologies is accelerated in the future.

The health and social care system will need to systematically identify and evaluate new technologies and medical advances, and promptly adopt and spread those of proven cost-effectiveness.

Making intelligent use of data and information

While the NHS is not short of data, far more could be done to make effective use of what exists and to support health and care professionals so that they can deliver safe and integrated care more easily. Data on clinical evidence have a crucial role in supporting treatment decisions. This includes, for example, the use of clinical decision support systems, treatment algorithms, and severity and risk scores to inform decisions about diagnosis, tests, and treatment, and to separate patients into clinically meaningful sub-groups to identify the most appropriate patient pathway (Bohmer 2011).

Data about clinical practice and patient outcomes has significant potential for enhancing service quality. Data of this kind can be benchmarked against peers and against evidence-based guidelines to identify areas where the quality of care is falling below standards, and then used to track progress in areas targeted for improvement. For example, when measuring compliance against protocols, rather than punishing clinicians whose practice vary from the protocol, high-performing organisations such as Intermountain Healthcare tend to regard such departures as learning opportunities and encourage physicians to record the reasons for this.

Kaiser Permanente's electronic patient care record compares patient information with evidence-based guidelines (Zhou *et al* 2010). This enables clinicians to identify any differences or 'gaps' between evidence-based recommendations and delivered care, including medication management, and any missed opportunities for timely screening and preventive care. For example, the system flags up if a patient with coronary artery disease has not filled out a prescription for a statin or ACE inhibitor for the past six months, or has no documentation for aspirin use (Liang *et al* 2010). The system also automatically identifies those patients with the greatest or most urgent gaps.

Electronic health records have the capability for recording more frequent and comprehensive data about an individual patients' health status, such as their vital statistics, and can automatically trigger alerts when these go outside of normal bounds. Making electronic records available to patients can help to support patient self-monitoring. As discussed, the recent information strategy (Department of Health 2012b) has set out an ambitious agenda for empowering patients through enabling them to access their own patient records electronically.

Data on the utilisation of services has significant potential for helping to predict future demand, in particular, levels of hospital admissions. If linked to information about a patient's lifestyle and attitudes to health, there is the potential for sophisticated risk stratification, allowing more anticipatory proactive care and targeted preventive services. Such data can also be used to target services and interventions at 'at risk' groups, thereby supporting the delivery of improved outcomes and the delivery of more care in the home and community settings.

At a population level, there is scope for epidemiological data on health, risk factors and behaviours to be linked to marketing data from other sources (eg, shopping loyalty cards) to provide a more rounded and sophisticated picture of habits and health profiles by postcode or even household. Such data could then be used to produce tailored health messages and information for local populations or individuals.

The health and social care system will be fit for the future when patients are given control of data about their health and care, and data are analysed in real time and fed back to those making decisions.

Summary

If the transformation of health and social care that is necessary to make the system fit for the future is to be realised, then we will need to challenge our thinking and the assumptions that underpin existing models of care. We will also need to look with fresh eyes at radically different approaches. The priority should be to strengthen those aspects of care that are working well and focus attention on addressing the weaknesses discussed in the previous section.

In this section we have explored a number of changes and areas of existing innovation that may hold potential for enhancing service quality and improving productivity:

- empowering patients to be partners in care
- making more effective use of the workforce and promoting effective team working
- delivering care closer to home or in the home, where appropriate
- fully using new information and communication technologies
- harnessing the potential of advances in medical science and technologies
- putting data and information in the hands of clinicians and patients.

In forthcoming work we will further explore the potential for these changes to achieve the transformation in care that is needed: incremental improvements will not be sufficient. We will also test out further what some of the principles should be to guide the design of future models of care. In the next section we consider how the process of innovation and change can best be supported.

4 Making it happen

If a sea change in the delivery of health and social care services is required to meet the needs of an ageing population and to respond to the changing burden of disease and rising public expectations, then how is this best achieved when public resources are unlikely to grow for the foreseeable future? Can new providers accelerate the adoption of innovations in care that are required to meet changing needs and to take advantage of the opportunities offered by new technologies? How realistic is it to expect public providers and commissioners to embrace innovation more effectively and more rapidly than in the past? And will an innovation strategy of the kind being proposed for the NHS be sufficient in view of the urgency facing the health and social care system?

In this final section of the paper, we move beyond outlining promising developments and areas of innovation to discuss what must be done to make them a reality.

Sources of innovation

The role of new providers

There has been increasing recognition of the need to do more to support innovation in the NHS. New providers have the potential to be a particularly important source of innovation, mirroring experience in other sectors where incumbent providers have found themselves challenged by start-ups whose business models have transformed how services are delivered to customers (budget airlines being a well-known example). The emphasis in the current NHS reforms on breaking down barriers to entry is intended in part to make it easier for new providers to be a source of innovation in future.

The difficulty in relying on new providers to be a major source of innovation is the track record of the NHS in commissioning from and referring to the private sector and the third sector. As an example, under the previous government, independent-sector treatment centres were intended to provide patients with a wider range of choices, but in many areas the capacity was underutilised, and primary care trusts were reluctant to take on the contracts. The contribution of these centres remains marginal, with the vast majority of elective and diagnostic care still delivered by NHS providers even though the evidence suggests that these independent-sector centres did make some contribution to the reductions in waiting times that occurred.

Much the same applies outside hospitals where new entrants into primary medical care and community health services have a limited role. The reasons for this include the barriers to entry facing new entrants, the time and costs of bidding for contracts, and the willingness of NHS commissioners to encourage new providers into the market. It remains to be seen whether clinical commissioning groups will support the emergence of a diverse range of providers and if they do, whether GPs will be willing to refer patients to them.

Change within the NHS

As well as encouraging new providers to enter the market, the current government recognised the need to support public sector providers to develop and spread innovative service models. A recent report to the NHS chief executive on ways of doing so set out an ambitious agenda that includes establishing a more systematic delivery mechanism for diffusion and collaboration within the NHS (Department of Health 2011b). The report recommended that the work of academic health sciences centres should be supported by the establishment of a number of academic health sciences networks, with the goal of improving population health and patient outcomes by translating research into practice. It was envisaged that networks would work with academic health sciences centres to identify high-impact innovations and spread their use at scale and pace.

Experience from other sectors contains clues on how to support the spread of innovation and the dissemination of good practice. A study of the experience of British Petroleum (BP) in the 1990s showed that a corporate culture in which managers were expected to lend support to their colleagues facing business challenges played an important part in the growth of the company during that period (Prokesch 1997). This suggests that the NHS needs to develop a culture that values peer support for learning and innovation.

A different example is the experience of General Electric (GE) in innovating by investing in emerging economies, a process known as 'reverse innovation' (Immelt *et al* 2009). This involved questioning conventional assumptions about the flow of innovation being from developed to developing economies. Instead, GE focused on developing high-quality and low-cost products such as ultrasound in China and India by establishing local growth teams in these countries and changing mindsets in the company's senior executives.

The challenge of innovation

There are three major challenges in achieving innovation within the NHS, whether through academic health sciences networks or other means.

System inertia

The first challenge is making change happen at scale and pace in an organisation as big and complex as the NHS. While recent improvements in performance demonstrate that change is possible, they have been achieved in a favourable financial climate and have taken time to deliver.

The NHS is now entering a decade of austerity, and we have argued in a previous paper that there is a need to focus on doing things differently and not just delivering more of the same (Appleby *et al* 2010). In our view inertia represents the greatest risk to the future of the NHS. Unless health and social care leaders are willing to embrace change and question established service models, the prospect is of a long-term decline in performance and a system that is increasingly unfit for purpose.

System inertia reflects the complexity of health systems generally (not only the NHS) and has been argued to be a natural response to an organisation facing many competing demands. It also illustrates experience of change management programmes, in both health care and other sectors, which often deliver far less than they promise because of the difficulty of changing established ways of working. This lies behind our concern that inbuilt inertia is the biggest risk to the NHS in the future.

One way of overcoming system inertia is to plan the destruction of redundant service models in order to create time and space to implement new ones. There is learning here from evolutionary processes in biology where programmed cell death (apoptosis) performs this function, as in the evolution of tadpoles into frogs (Coiera 2011). The need to find more effective ways of decommissioning public services applies across the public sector as Nesta has argued in an analysis of case studies drawn from health care and other services (Bunt and Leadbeater 2012).

The example of mental health services is again relevant, illustrating that major change is possible provided that funding arrangements enable new services to be established as old ones are removed. In this case, a vision of care being delivered in the community played a key role in supporting the changes that occurred, and this was linked to national leadership by politicians and local leadership by managers and clinicians. Although many challenges were encountered along the way, over a period of 20 years a new model of care was implemented in line with this vision.

Complex adaptive systems

The second challenge is that health care systems are complex adaptive systems and unlike mechanical systems, they cannot always be planned and controlled in a meaningful way. Complex adaptive systems are made up of individuals and sub-systems whose interactions are hard to predict, resulting in variations in practice and performance that make it difficult to spread innovations between settings and organisations. Although some variations may be unwarranted (Appleby *et al* 2011), others may be desirable as a way of testing and discovering new models of care.

Linear models of change, such as those proposed in the recent review of innovation in the NHS (Department of Health 2011b), may deliver less than they promise if they fail to work with the grain of the NHS as a complex adaptive system. The dilemma here is how to marry understanding of complexity and the many factors that bear on 'the sustainability, decay, spread, and containment of new working practices' (Buchanan *et al* 2007) with the urgency of making the fundamental changes we have outlined. While there is 'no simple policy directive or effortless management strategy to guarantee either the durability of new working practices or their wide and rapid spread' (Buchanan *et al* 2007), it is clear that more widespread and rapid innovation is needed.

As we have argued in other work (The King's Fund 2012b), the answer lies in part in finding more effective ways of engaging staff at all levels in developing new ways of delivering care and empowering them to make changes. There is evidence from social enterprises and employee-owned companies that the key to their success is the ability to engage staff, rather than the ownership model per se (Addicott 2011). Another promising approach is to seek to build a social movement for change in which innovation occurs by harnessing the creativity, energy and commitment of those working in the NHS, recognising their intrinsic motivation to provide high-quality care that meets the needs of patients and service users (Bibby *et al* 2009). The development of the NHS Change Model is an attempt to translate the theory of social movements into practical programmes that make a difference on a large scale.

Risk-taking

The third challenge is the attitude to risk-taking in the NHS, and public services more generally. The culture of centrally driven performance management has placed a premium on delivering targets set by government, and has not encouraged leaders at a local level to test new models of care. The experience of NHS Foundation Trusts is instructive in this regard with most of these organisations being slow to make use of the freedoms they were given, leading the former Chairman of Monitor to bemoan the culture of the NHS and the way in which it inhibited innovation (Timmins 2010).

The unwillingness of NHS organisations to depart from established ways of working has militated against the approach advocated by Harford (2011) and others of active experimentation through which success emerges out of failure. Unless politicians are prepared to move decisively away from this culture, and leaders at a local level are prepared to use the freedoms available to them, then conformity rather than experimentation will continue to be the norm. In these circumstances, the NHS will not be able to make changes to the delivery of care on the scale and at the pace that the challenges facing public services demand.

The way forward

For all of these reasons, implementing the transformational changes we have advocated will be difficult. Not only is there no magic bullet, but also there are major challenges in supporting the kinds of innovations that are needed. Addressing these challenges is likely to require the use of a bundle of interventions that together comprise 'a complex of coherent actions that both build and destroy' (Coiera 2011).

An approach that facilitates new providers to enter the market, as well as enabling existing providers to try different approaches is essential if the health and social care system is going to adapt to changing needs and demands. As we have argued, this may require greater attention to the planned destruction of older service models, or at least their re-invention, to enable new ones to become established. Exit, in other words, is a precondition for entry and arguably for survival.

Leadership of the highest order is required to make this happen both locally and nationally. Within the NHS, leaders must be more effective in identifying and copying best practice wherever it exists. This includes looking outside their organisations and being willing to adapt tried and tested ideas and approaches developed by others, especially when there is a high degree of certainty about the best way of providing care. The systematic adoption of best practices, where evidence on how to provide high-quality care is sound, is a characteristic of high-performing health care organisations.

At a national level the approach taken by the NHS Commissioning Board must reflect understanding of the NHS as a complex adaptive system and the limits to command and control. Central to this is an approach to commissioning that focuses on the outcomes of care across the whole pathway or system of care to enable different organisations to work together to achieve innovations and improvements. For their part, politicians must be willing to support risk-taking and experimentation in the full knowledge that sometimes this will result in failure.

Innovation in complex adaptive systems is often best achieved by harnessing the creativity and skills of the people in these systems, rather than seeking to mandate change through an organisational hierarchy. The seminal analysis conducted by the Institute of Medicine suggested that this can be done by setting some 'simple rules' to guide behaviour in the 21st-century health care system, as illustrated in Table 1, overleaf. Plsek and Wilson (2001) have applied this approach to the NHS and have argued that leaders need to focus on the operation of the whole system instead of parts of the system if they are to bring about lasting improvements in performance.

The potential of reverse innovation should also be explored. In the previous section, we cited the example of the Aravind Eye Care System in India to illustrate new ways of using staff to deliver care in emerging economies. Radically different models of care are likely to depend on NHS and social care organisations emulating the approach taken by GE (*see* p 39) and finding ways of learning from experience and adapting innovations that emerge in countries like India and China.

Table 1 Simple rules for the health care system of the 21st century

Current approach	New rule
Care is based primarily on visits	Care is based on continuous healing relationships
Professional autonomy drives variability	Care is customised according to patient needs and values
Professionals control care	The patient is the source of control
Information is a record	Knowledge is shared and information flows freely
Decision-making is based on training and experience	Decision-making is evidence-based
'Do no harm' is an individual responsibility	Safety is a system property
Secrecy is necessary	Transparency is necessary
The system reacts to needs	Needs are anticipated
Cost reduction is sought	Waste is continuously decreased
Preference is given to professional roles over the system	Co-operation among clinicians is a priority

Source: Committee on Quality of Health Care in America, Institute of Medicine (2001).

Although difficult, transformational change in health care organisations is not without precedent. The turnaround of the VA in the United States, discussed on p 31, is one of the best-known examples, involving the transformation of a large public health care system over a five-year period. This was achieved through a number of inter-related actions including agreement on a new vision for the VA, implementation of a structure to help achieve the vision, and the appointment of the right people to make it happen. As this example confirms, transformational change hinges on a bundle of interventions rather than a magic bullet, as well as a willingness to persist in the face of inevitable obstacles along the way.

There will be some who will contend that a much bolder and more radical approach is needed to deal with the challenges that lie ahead, arguing in the time-honoured phrase that 'desperate times require desperate measures'. While we are sympathetic to this point of view, and have drawn on it in making the case for fundamental reform of the delivery system, we are also conscious that national and local leaders face the task of moving in the direction of the desirable future system bearing the legacy of a multitude of past investment and planning decisions. In these circumstances, starting with a blank sheet of paper is simply not an option, and the focus needs to be on finding ways of innovating that recognise the reality of this legacy, the complexity of change management in the NHS, and the urgency of making change happen.

To make this point is to emphasise that the broken delivery system will only be fixed if as much attention is given to the means of change as to the endpoint to be reached. Discussion of innovation, implementation and execution may be distinctly unfashionable compared with debate about new models of care, and yet they are of fundamental importance in setting out a credible plan for the future. The work of Govindarajan and Trimble (2010) places particular emphasis on skills in execution as the critical ingredient in innovation, rather than the search for the next big idea. To invoke a well-known adage, there is no such thing as an implementation gap, only policies and strategies that are poorly designed and do not allow for the realities of implementation.

Using this insight, we would contend that the leaders of the health and social care system need to match visions to resources and find more effective ways of turning those visions into practice. Strengthening capacities and capabilities for change and supporting those leading health and social care to re-invent services in the ways set out in this paper are therefore critical requirements. This includes communicating with politicians and the public as to why fundamental change is needed, and setting out a compelling vision of how the future will be both different and better. We hope the case for change we set out here will garner wide support from politicians and health and social care leaders and enable us all to think differently about how to deliver health and social care in the future.

References

Addicott R (2011). *Social Enterprise in Health Care: Promoting organisational autonomy and staff engagement.* London: The King's Fund. Available at: www.kingsfund.org.uk/publications/social_enterprise_in.html (accessed on 17 July 2012).

Altogether Better (2008–12). Altogether Better website. Available at: www.altogetherbetter.org.uk/ (accessed on 19 July 2012).

Appleby J (2012). 'A productivity challenge too far?' *British Medical Journal*, vol 344, e2416.

Appleby J, Ham C, Imison C, Jennings M (2010). *Improving NHS Productivity: More with the same not more of the same.* London: The King's Fund. Available at: www.kingsfund.org.uk/publications/improving_nhs.html (accessed on 17 July 2012).

Appleby J, Raleigh V, Frosini F, Bevan G. Gao H, Lyscom T (2011). *Variations in Health Care: The good, the bad, and the inexplicable.* London: The King's Fund. Available at: www.kingsfund.org.uk/publications/healthcare_variation.html (accessed on 17 July 2012).

Association of Directors of Adult Social Services (2012). *ADASS Budget Survey 2012.* London: ADASS. Available at: www.adass.org.uk/images/stories/Press12/ADASS_BudgetSurvey2012Summary.pdf (accessed on 9 July 2012).

Audit Commission (2003). *Bed Management: Review of national findings.* London: Audit Commission. Available at: www.audit-commission.gov.uk/nationalstudies/health/other/pages/bedmanagement.aspx (accessed on 17 July 2012).

Barnett K, Mercer S, Norbury M, Watt G, Wyke S, Guthrie B (2012). 'Epidemiology of multimorbidity and implications for health care, research, and medical education: a cross-sectional study'. *The Lancet*, vol 380, no 9836, pp 37–43.

Bibby J, Bevan H, Carter E, Bate P, Robert G (2009). *The Power of One, the Power of Many: Bringing social movement thinking to health and healthcare improvement.* Warwick: Institute of Innovation and Improvement.

Bohmer RMJ (2011). 'The four habits of high-value health care organizations'. *The New England Journal of Medicine*, vol 365, pp 2045–7.

British Red Cross (2012). 'Dangerous cuts are putting vulnerable people at risk'. British Red Cross website. Available at: www.redcross.org.uk/About-us/News/2012/June/Dangerous-cuts-are-putting-vulnerable-people-at-risk (accessed on 9 July 2012).

Buchanan D, Fitzgerald L, Ketley D (2007). *The Sustainability and Spread of Organizational Change.* London: Routledge.

Bunt L, Leadbeater C (2012). *The Art of Exit: In search of creative decommissioning.* London: Nesta. Available at: www.nesta.org.uk/publications/assets/features/the_art_of_exit (accessed on 17 July 2012).

Care Quality Commission (2011). *Dignity and Nutrition: Inspection programme.* Newcastle upon Tyne: CQC. Available at: www.cqc.org.uk/public/reports-surveys-and-reviews/themes-inspections/dignity-and-nutrition-older-people (accessed on 17 July 2012).

Center for Health Enhancement Systems Studies (2012). 'Current studies and projects'. CHESS website. Available at: http://chess.wisc.edu/chess/projects/current_studies_and_projects.aspx (accessed on 19 July 2012).

Centre for Workforce Intelligence (2012). *Shape of the Medical Workforce: Starting the debate on the future consultant workforce: A discussion document for leaders.* London: CFYI. Available at: www.cfwi.org.uk/publications/leaders-report-shape-of-the-medical-workforce (accessed on 17 July 2012).

Chen C, Garrido T, Chock D, Okawa G, Liang L (2009). 'The Kaiser Permanente electronic health record: transforming and streamlining modalities of care'. *Health Affairs*, vol 28, no 2, pp 323–3.

Christensen C, Bohmer R, Kenagy J (2000). 'Will disruptive innovations cure health care?' *Harvard Business Review*, vol 78, no 5, pp 102–12, 199.

Christensen K, Silvestre A-L (2010). 'Making health personal' in Liang LL (ed), *Connected for Health. Using electronic health records to transform care delivery.* NJ: Jossey-Bass.

Coiera E (2011). 'Why system inertia makes health reform so difficult'. *British Medical Journal*, vol 342, d3693.

Committee on Quality of Health Care in America, Institute of Medicine (2001). *Crossing the Quality Chasm: A new health system for the 21st century.* Washington, DC: National Academy Press.

Cornwell J, Levenson R, Sonolo L, Poteliakhoff E (2012). *Continuity of Care for Older Hospital Patients: A call for action.* London: The King's Fund. Available at: www.kingsfund.org.uk/publications/continuity_of_care.html (accessed on16 July 2012).

Coulter A (2012). *Leadership for Patient Engagement.* London: The King's Fund. Available at: www.kingsfund.org.uk/leadershipreview (accessed on 17 July 2012).

Coulter A, Richards N (2007). *Is the NHS Becoming More Patient-Centred? Trends from the national surveys of NHS patients in England 2002–07.* Oxford: Picker Institute.

CSC Leading Edge Forum (2010). *The Future of Healthcare: It's health, then care.* Falls Church, VA: Computer Science Corporation (CSC).

Davidson J, Baxter K, Glendinning C, Jones K, Forder J, Caiels J, Welch E, Windle K, Dolan P, King D (2012). *Personal Health Budgets: Experiences and outcomes for budget holders at nine months. Fifth interim report.* London: Department of Health.

Davis K, Schoen C, Stremikis K (2010). *Mirror, Mirror on the Wall. How the Performance of the U.S. Health Care System Compares Internationally.* 2010 Update. New York, NY: The Commonwealth Fund.

Department of Health (2012a). *Long Term Conditions Compendium of Information,* 3rd ed. London: Department of Health. Available at: www.dh.gov.uk/prod_consum_dh/groups/dh_digitalassets/@dh/@en/documents/digitalasset/dh_134486.pdf (accessed on 17 July 2012).

Department of Health (2012b). *The Power of Information: Putting all of us in control of the health and care information we need.* London: Department of Health. Available at: www.dh.gov.uk/en/Publicationsandstatistics/Publications/PublicationsPolicyAndGuidance/DH_134181 (accessed on 17 July 2012).

Department of Health (2011a). *Improving Outcomes: A strategy for cancer.* London: Department of Health. Available at: www.dh.gov.uk/en/Publicationsandstatistics/Publications/PublicationsPolicyAndGuidance/DH_123371 (accessed on 17 July 2012).

Department of Health (2011b). *Innovation, Health and Wealth. Accelerating adoption and diffusion in the NHS.* London: Department of Health.

Department of Health (2010). 'Average daily number of available beds, by sector, England, 1987–88 to 2009–10'. Department of Health website. Available at: www.dh.gov.uk/prod_consum_dh/groups/dh_digitalassets/@dh/@en/@ps/@sta/@perf/documents/digitalasset/dh_133690.xls (accessed on 6 July 2012).

Department of Health (2009). *Living Well with Dementia: A national dementia strategy.* London: Department of Health. Available at: www.dh.gov.uk/en/Publicationsandstatistics/Publications/PublicationsPolicyAndGuidance/DH_094058 (accessed on 17 July 2012).

Department of Health (2008). *Healthy Foundations: A segmentation model.* London: Department of Health. Available at: www.dh.gov.uk/prod_consum_dh/groups/dh_digitalassets/documents/digitalasset/dh_086291.pdf (accessed on 27 June 2012).

Department of Health (2007). *Our NHS Our Future: NHS next stage review. Interim report.* London: Department of Health. Available at: www.dh.gov.uk/en/Publicationsandstatistics/Publications/PublicationsPolicyAndGuidance/DH_079077 (accessed on 17 July 2012).

Diabetes UK, Department of Health, The Health Foundation, NHS Diabetes (2011). *Year of Care: Report of findings from the pilot programme.* Available at: www.diabetes.nhs.uk/document.php?o=2926 (accessed on 9 July 2012).

Dixon A, Tian Y, Gao H (2012). *Emergency Hospital Admissions for Ambulatory Care-Sensitive Conditions: Identifying the potential for reductions.* London: The King's Fund. Available at: www.kingsfund.org.uk/publications/data_briefing.html (accessed on 17 July 2012).

Dr Foster Intelligence (2011). *Inside your hospital. Dr Foster Hospital Guide. 2001–2011.* Available at: http://drfosterintelligence.co.uk/wp-content/uploads/2011/11/Hospital_Guide_2011.pdf (accessed on 9 July 2012).

Goddard M, McDonagh M, Smith D (2000). 'Avoidable Use of Beds and Cost-Effectiveness of Care in Alternative Locations' in Department of Health, *Shaping the future NHS: long term planning for hospitals and related services. Consultation document on the findings of the National Beds Inquiry – supporting analysis*, pp 96–101. London: Department of Health.

Govindarajan V, Trimble C (2010). *The Other Side of Innovation: Solving the execution challenge.* Boston, MA: Harvard Business Press.

Harford T (2011). *Adapt: Why success always starts with failure.* London: Little, Brown.

Hawe E, Yuen P, Baillie L (2011). *OHE Guide to UK Health and Health Care Statistics.* London: Office of Health Economics.

The Health Foundation (2012). *Snapshot: MAGIC: Making good decisions in collaboration.* London: The Health Foundation. Available at: www.health.org.uk/publications/snapshot-magic/ (accessed on 17 July 2012).

HM Government (2012). *Caring for our Future: Progress report on funding reform.* Cm 8381. London: The Stationery Office. Available at: www.dh.gov.uk/health/files/2012/07/progress-report-on-social-care-funding-reform-Accessible-version1.pdf (accessed on 14 August 2012).

House of Commons Health Committee (2009). *Health Committee Sixth Report: Patient safety.* London: House of Commons.

Housing Learning and Improvement Network, Association of Directors of Adult Social Services (2011). *Strategic Housing for Older People: Planning, designing and delivering housing that older people want.* London: Housing Learning and Improvement Network.

Hughes-Hallett T, Craft A, Davies C (2011). *Palliative Care Funding Review. Funding the Right Care and Support for Everyone. Creating a Fair and Transparent Funding System; the Final Report of the Palliative Care Funding Review* [online]. Available at: http://palliativecarefunding.org.uk/PCFRFinal%20Report.pdf (accessed on 9 July 2012).

Humphries R (2011). *Social Care Funding and the NHS: An impending crisis?* London: The King's Fund. Available at: www.kingsfund.org.uk/publications/social_care_funding.html (accessed on 17 July 2012).

Imison C, Naylor C, Maybin J (2008). *Under One Roof: Will polyclinics deliver integrated care?* London: The King's Fund. Available at: www.kingsfund.org.uk/publications/under_one_roof.html (accessed on 17 July 2012).

Imison C, Poteliakhoff E, Thompson J (2012). *Older People and Emergency Bed Use: Exploring variation.* London: The King's Fund.

Immelt JR, Govindarajan V, Trimble C (2009). 'How GE is disrupting itself'. *Harvard Business Review*, October. Available at: www.antoniovidigal.com/drupal/cd/sites/all/PDFs/how_ge_is_disrupting_itself%5B1%5D.pdf (accessed on 9 July 2012).

Improvement and Development Agency (2010). *A Glass Half-full: how an asset approach can improve community health and well-being.* London: IDEA. Available at: www.bankofideas.com.au/Downloads/GlassHalfFull.pdf (accessed on 9 July 2012).

Institute for Healthcare Improvement (2012). *A Community. IHI Progress Report 2012.* Cambridge MA: IHI.

King's College London, London School of Economics (2007). *Dementia UK: The full report.* London: Alzheimer's Society. Available at: http://alzheimers.org.uk/site/scripts/download_info.php?fileID=2 (accessed on 17 July 2012).

The King's Fund (2012a). 'Experience-based co-design: working with patients to improve health care'. Toolkit. The King's Fund website. Available at: www.kingsfund.org.uk/ebcd/introduction.html (accessed on 19 July 2012).

The King's Fund (2012b). *Leadership and Engagement for Improvement in the NHS: Together we can.* London: The King's Fund. Available at: www.kingsfund.org.uk/publications/leadership_review_12.html (accessed on 17 July 2012).

The King's Fund (2011). *Improving the Quality of Care in General Practice: Report of an independent inquiry commissioned by The King's Fund.* London: The King's Fund. Available at: www.kingsfund.org.uk/publications/gp_inquiry_report.html (accessed on 17 July 2012).

Kizer K (2001). 'Re-engineering the Veterans Healthcare System' in Ramsaroop P (ed), *Advancing Federal Sector Health Care.* New York: Springer-Verlag.

Lakey L (2009). *Counting the Cost. Caring for people with dementia on hospital wards.* London: Alzheimer's Society. Available at: http://alzheimers.org.uk/countingthecost/ (accessed on 17 July 2012).

Laurant MJ, Harmsen M, Faber M, Wollersheim H, Sibbauld B, Grol R (2010). *Revision of Professional Roles and Quality Improvement: A review of the evidence.* London: The Health Foundation.

Law Commission (2011). *Adult Social Care.* London: The Stationery Office.

Liang LL (2010). *Connected for Health. Using electronic health records to transform care delivery.* Hoboken, NJ: Jossey-Bass.

Liang LL, Unitan R, Weissberg J (2010). 'Managing the health of populations' in Liang LL (ed), *Connected for Health. Using electronic health records to transform care delivery*, pp 109–26. Hoboken, NJ: Jossey-Bass.

Local Government Association, NHS Confederation, Age UK (2012). *Delivering Dignity: Securing dignity in care for older people in hospitals and care homes.* Available at: www.nhsconfed.org/Documents/dignity.pdf (accessed on 9 July 2012).

London School of Economics and Political Science (2012). *How Mental Illness Loses out in the NHS: A report by the Centre for Economic Performance's Mental Health Policy Group.* London: LSE. Available at: http://cep.lse.ac.uk/_new/research/mentalhealth/default.asp (accessed on 17 July 2012).

Marmot M (2010). *Fair Society, Healthy Lives.* London: The Marmot Review. Available at: www.instituteofhealthequity.org/projects/fair-society-healthy-lives-the-marmot-review (accessed on 9 July 2012).

Mental Health Strategies (2011). *2010/11 National Survey of Investment in Adult Mental Health Services.* London: Department of Health.

Mind (2010). *We Need to Talk: Getting the right therapy at the right time.* London: Mind. Available at: www.mind.org.uk/assets/0001/0027/Mind_We_need_to_talk_Report.pdf (accessed on 9 July 2012).

Mirnezami R, Nicholson J, Darzi A (2012). 'Preparing for precision medicine'. *The New England Journal of Medicine*, vol 366, pp 489–91.

Mulley A, Trimble C, Elwyn G (2012). *Patients' Preferences Matter: Stop the silent misdiagnosis.* London: The King's Fund. Available at: www.kingsfund.org.uk/publications/patients_preferences.html (accessed on 17 July 2012).

Munton T, Martin A, Marrero I, Llewellyn A, Gibson K, Gomersall A (2011). *Getting Out of Hospital? The evidence for shifting acute inpatient and day case services from hospitals into the community.* London: The Health Foundation.

National Audit Office (2012). *The Management of Adult Diabetes Services in the NHS.* London: National Audit Office. Available at: www.nao.org.uk/publications/1213/adult_diabetes_services.aspx (accessed on 17 July 2012).

National Audit Office (2010a). *Improving Dementia Services in England – An interim report.* London: The Stationery Office. Available at: www.nao.org.uk/publications/0910/improving_dementia_services.aspx (accessed on 17 July 2012).

National Audit Office (2010b). *Management of NHS Hospital Productivity.* London: The Stationery Office. Available at: www.nao.org.uk/publications/1011/nhs_hospital_productivity.aspx (accessed on 17 July 2012).

National Confidential Enquiry into Patient Outcome and Death (2007). *Emergency Admissions: A journey in the right direction?* London: NCEPOD. Available at: www.ncepod.org.uk/2007ea.htm (accessed on 14 August 2012).

National End of Life Care Programme (2012). *Deaths from Liver Disease: Implications for end of life care in England.* Leicester: National End of Life Intelligence Network. Available at: www.endoflifecare-intelligence.org.uk/resources/publications/deaths_from_liver_disease.aspx (accessed on 9 July 2012).

National Obesity Observatory (2011). 'Examining available data for the adult population' (Adult slide set). National Obesity Observatory website. Available at: www.noo.org.uk/NOO_about_obesity/ (accessed on 9 July 2012).

Naylor C, Bell A (2010). *Mental Health and the Productivity Challenge: Improving quality and value for money.* London: The King's Fund. Available at: www.kingsfund.org.uk/publications/mental_health_and.html (accessed on 17 July 2012).

Naylor C, Parsonage M, McDaid D, Knapp M, Fossey M, Galea A (2012). *Long-Term Conditions and Mental Health: The cost of co-morbidities.* London: The King's Fund. Available at: www.kingsfund.org.uk/publications/mental_health_ltcs.html (accessed on 17 July 2012).

Naylor R, Wyatt M, Mitchell D (2012). 'High volume surgery outcomes suggest there is safety in numbers'. *Health Service Journal,* 8 March. Available at: www.hsj.co.uk/opinion/columnists/high-volume-surgery-outcomes-suggest-there-is-safety-in-numbers/5042184.article (accessed on 9 July 2012).

Netten A, Darton R, Bäumker T, Callaghan, L. (2011) *Improving Housing with Care Choices for Older People: An evaluation of extra care housing.* Canterbury: University of Kent Personal Social Services Research Unit.

NHS Diabetes (2012). 'Year of Care: Working together for better healthcare and better self care'. NHS Diabetes website. Available at: www.diabetes.nhs.uk/year_of_care/ (accessed on 19 July 2012).

NHS Information Centre (2012). *Community Care Statistics 2010–11: Social services activity report, England.* Leeds: NHS Information Centre. Available at: www.ic.nhs.uk/pubs/finalcarestats1011ssa (accessed on 17 July 2012).

NHS Information Centre (2011a). *Health Survey for England 2010: Trend tables.* Leeds: NHS Information Centre. Available at: www.ic.nhs.uk/statistics-and-data-collections/health-and-lifestyles-related-surveys/health-survey-for-england/health-survey-for-england--2010-trend-tables (accessed on 17 July 2012).

NHS Information Centre (2011b). *Personal Social Services Adult Social Care Survey, England 2010–11: Final release.* Leeds: NHS Information Centre. Available at: www.ic.nhs.uk/statistics-and-data-collections/social-care/adult-social-care-information/personal-social-services-adult-social-care-survey-england--final-2010-11 (accessed on 17 July 2012).

NHS London (2011). *Adult Emergency Services: Acute medicine and emergency general surgery: Case for change.* London: NHS London. Available at: www.londonhp.nhs.uk/wp-content/uploads/2011/09/AES-Case-for-change_September-2011.pdf (accessed on 9 July 2012).

NHS RightCare (2011). *The Atlas of Variation in Healthcare: Reducing unwarranted variation to increase value and improve quality* [online]. Available at: http://www.rightcare.nhs.uk/index.php/atlas/atlas-of-variation-2011/ (accessed on 19 July 2012).

NHS RightCare (2010). *The Atlas of Variation in Healthcare: Reducing unwarranted variation to increase value and improve quality* [online]. Available at: www.rightcare.nhs.uk/index.php/atlas/atlas-of-variation-2010/ (accessed 14 August 2012).

Nicholson D (2012). *The Year: NHS Chief Executive's annual report 2011/12, including The Quarter, Quarter 4 2011/12*. London: Department of Health. Available at: www.wp.dh.gov.uk/health/files/2012/06/the-year-and-quarter-4-210612-gw-17802-PDF-2.33MB.pdf (accessed on 9 July 2012).

Nolte E, McKee M (2011). 'Variations in amenable mortality – trends in 16 high-income nations'. *Health Policy*, vol 103 no 1, pp 47–52.

Office for National Statistics (2012). *Pension Trends. Chapter 2: Population change*. Available at: www.ons.gov.uk/ons/rel/pensions/pension-trends/chapter-2--population-change--2012-edition-/index.html (accessed on 9 July 2012).

Office for National Statistics (2011a). *2010-based National Population Projections*. Available at: www.ons.gov.uk/ons/rel/npp/national-population-projections/2010-based-projections/index.html (accessed on 9 July 2012).

Office for National Statistics (2011b). *2010-based Period and Cohort Life Expectancy Tables*. Available at: www.ons.gov.uk/ons/rel/lifetables/period-and-cohort-life-expectancy-tables/2010-based/p-and-c-le.html (accessed on 22 August 2012).

Office for National Statistics (2011c). *Estimates of Centenarians in the UK*. Available at: www.ons.gov.uk/ons/dcp171780_233627.pdf (accessed on 9 July 2012).

Office for National Statistics (2011d). *Health Expectancies in the United Kingdom, 2000–2002 to 2007–2009*. Available at: www.ons.gov.uk/ons/taxonomy/index.html?nscl=Health+Expectancy (accessed on 14 August 2012).

Office for National Statistics (2011e). *Population Estimates for UK, England and Wales, Scotland and Northern Ireland Mid-2010*. Available at: www.ons.gov.uk/ons/rel/pop-estimate/population-estimates-for-uk--england-and-wales--scotland-and-northern-ireland/mid-2010-population-estimates/index.html (accessed on 14 August 2012).

Office for National Statistics (2011f). *Social Trends 41 – Health data*. Available at: www.ons.gov.uk/ons/publications/re-reference-tables.html?edition=tcm%3A77-218733 (accessed on 9 July 2012).

Office for National Statistics (2011g). *Statistical Bulletin. Internet Access 2010: Households and Individuals*. Available at: www.ons.gov.uk/ons/rel/rdit2/internet-access---households-and-individuals/2011/stb-internet-access-2011.html (accessed on 9 July 2012).

Office for National Statistics (2004). *Health Expectancies at birth and age 65 in the United Kingdom, 1981–2001*. Available at: http://www.ons.gov.uk/ons/rel/disability-and-health-measurement/health-expectancies-at-birth-and-age-65-in-the-united-kingdom/1981-2001/index.html (accessed on 19 July 2012).

Organisation for Economic Co-operation and Development (2012). *Obesity and the Economics of Prevention. Fit not fat. Key facts England Update 2012*. Available at: www.oecd.org/dataoecd/0/61/49712153.pdf (accessed on 9 July 2012).

Organisation for Economic Co-operation and Development (2011). *Health at a Glance 2011: OECD Indicators*. Available at: www.oecd.org/dataoecd/6/28/49105858.pdf (accessed on 9 July 2012).

Organisation for Economic Co-operation and Development (2009). *Health Care Quality Indicators*. Available at: www.oecd.org/document/34/0,3746,en_2649_37407_37088930_1_1_1_37407,00.html (accessed on 9 July 2012).

Pannell J, Aldridge H, Kenway P (2012). *Older People's Housing: Choice, quality of life and under-occupation.* York: Joseph Rowntree Foundation. Available at: www.jrf.org.uk/publications/older-peoples-housing-choice (accessed on 17 July 2012).

Plsek PE, Wilson T (2001). 'Complexity, leadership and management in health care organisations'. *British Medical Journal*, vol 323, 746.1.

Poteliakhoff E, Thompson J (2011). *Emergency Bed Use: What the numbers tell us.* London: The King's Fund. Available at: www.kingsfund.org.uk/publications/emergency_bed_use.html (accessed on 17 July 2012).

Prokesch S (1997). 'Unleashing the power of learning: an interview with British Petroleum's John Browne'. *Harvard Business Review*, vol 75, no 5, pp 147–68.

Purdy S (2010). *Avoiding Hospital Admissions: What does the research evidence say?* London: The King's Fund. Available at: www.kingsfund.org.uk/publications/avoiding_hospital.html (accessed on 17 July 2012).

Realpe A, Wallace L M (2010). *What Is Co-production?* London: The Health Foundation. Available at: www.health.org.uk/media_manager/public/75/SMS_resource-centre_publications/What%20is%20co-production.pdf (accessed on 17 July 2012).

Richards M (2009). 'The size of the prize for earlier diagnosis of cancer in England'. *British Journal of Cancer*, vol 101, suppl 2, pp S125–9.

Royal College of Physicians (2012). *An Evaluation of Consultant Input into Acute Medical Admissions Management in England.* Report of: Hospital service patterns versus clinical outcomes in England. London: RCP. Available at: www.rcplondon.ac.uk/sites/default/files/an-evaluation-of-consultant-input-into-acute-medical-admissions-management-in-england-2012.pdf (accessed on 9 July 2012).

Royal College of Physicians, Royal College of General Practitioners, Royal College of Paediatrics and Child Health (2008). *Teams without Walls: Working together will improve patient care.* London: Royal College of Physicians. Available at: www.bacch.org.uk/publications/documents/teams-without-walls.pdf (accessed on 9 July 2012).

Sandall J, Homer C, Sadler E, Rudisill C, Bourgeault I, Bewley S, Nelson P, Cowie L, Cooper C, Curry N (2011). *Staffing in Maternity Units: Getting the right people in the right place at the right time.* London: The King's Fund. Available at: www.kingsfund.org.uk/publications/maternity_unit_staff.html (accessed on 17 July 2012).

Sandwell and West Birmingham Hospitals Trust (2009). *Outline Business Case: Towards 2010 Programme Acute Hospital Development.* Available at: www.swbh.nhs.uk/documents/obc.pdf (accessed on 9 July 2012).

Schoen C, Osborn R, How S, Doty M, Peugh J (2009). 'In chronic condition: experiences of patients with complex health care needs, in eight countries, 2008'. *Health Affairs (Millwood)*, vol 28, no 1, pp w1–16.

Skills for Care (2010). *The State of the Adult Social Care Workforce in England, 2010.* Leeds: Skills for Care. Available at: www.skillsforcare.org.uk/research/research_reports/state_of_the_adult_social_care_workforce_reports.aspx (accessed on 17 July 2012).

Smith MP, Olatunde O, White C (2011). 'Disability-free life expectancy: comparison of sources and small area estimates in England, 2006–08'. *Health Statistics Quarterly*, no 50. Available at: www.ons.gov.uk/ons/rel/hsq/health-statistics-quarterly/no--50--summer-2011/index.html

Snell T, Wittenberg R, Fernandez J, Malley J, Comas-Herrera A, King D (2011). *Projections of Demand for Social Care and Disability Benefits for Younger Adults in England. Report of Research Conducted for the Commission on Funding of Care and Support. PSSRU Discussion paper 2800/3*. London: Economics of Social and Health Care Research Unit. Available at: www.pssru.ac.uk/pdf/DP2880-3.pdf (accessed on 9 July 2012).

South J, Raine G, White J (2010). *Community Health Champions: Evidence review*. Centre for Health Promotion, Leeds Metropolitan University. Available at: www.yhpho.org.uk/resource/view.aspx?RID=8749 (accessed on 9 July 2012).

Starfield B (1998). *Primary Care: Balancing health needs, services and technology*. Oxford: Oxford University Press.

Steventon A, Bardsley M (2012). *The Impact of Telehealth on Use of Hospital Care and Mortality: A summary of first findings from the Whole System Demonstrator trial*. London: Nuffield Trust.

Taylor J (ed) (2012). 'Out of hospital care: from vision to reality'. *HSJ Service Provision, an HSJ Supplement*, 21 June. Available at: www.hsj.co.uk/Journals/2012/06/25/t/s/b/BUPA-supplement.pdf (accessed on 9 July 2012).

Thistlethwaite P (2011). *Integrating Health and Social Care in Torbay: Improving care for Mrs Smith*. London: The King's Fund. Available at: www.kingsfund.org.uk/publications/integrating_health_1.html (accessed on 17 July 2012).

Thompson R (2011). 'Delivering a 7 Day Hospital: Ensuring consultant-led service 7 days a week' [slide set]. Available at: www.healthcareconferencesuk.co.uk/presentations/downloads/Sir_Richard_Thompson.pdf (accessed 14 August 2012).

Thorlby R, Maybin J (2010). *A High Performing NHS? A review of progress 1997–2010*. London: The King's Fund. Available at: www.kingsfund.org.uk/publications/a_highperforming_nh.html (accessed on 17 July 2012).

Timmins N (2010). 'Health department still sees itself as "HQ of the hospital system," says former regulator'. *British Medical Journal*, vol 340, c1405.

Tudor-Hart J (1971). 'The inverse care law'. *The Lancet*, vol 1, no 7696, pp 405–12.

Wang C, McPherson K, Marsh T, Gortmaker S, Brown M. (2011). 'Health and economic burden of the projected obesity trends in the USA and the UK'. *The Lancet*, vol 378, no 9793, pp 815–25.

Wanless D (2006). *Securing Good Care for Older People. Taking a long-term view*. London: The King's Fund. Available at: www.kingsfund.org.uk/publications/securing_good.html (accessed on 17 July 2012).

Watcher R, Bell D (2012). 'Renaissance of hospital generalists'. *British Medical Journal*, vol 344, p e652.

Wittenberg R, Hu B, Hancock R, Morciano M, Comas-Herrera A, Malley J, King D (2011). *Projections of Demand for and Costs of Social Care for Older People in England, 2010 to 2030, under Current and Alternative Funding Systems. Report of research for the Commission on Funding of Care and Support*. Canterbury and London: PSSRU, University of Kent and London School of Economics. Available at: http://eprints.lse.ac.uk/40720/1/2811-2.pdf (accessed on 9 July 2012).

Wolfe I, Cass H, Thompson MJ, Craft A, Peile E, Wiegersma PA, Janson S, Chambers TL, McKee M. (2011). 'Improving child health services in the UK: insights from Europe and their implications for the NHS reforms'. *British Medical Journal*, vol 342, d1277.

Woodall J, Kinsella K, South K, White J (2012). *Community Health Champions and Older People: A review of the evidence. A report commissioned by the Altogether Better Network.* Available at: www.altogetherbetter.org.uk/evidence-and-resources (accessed on 9 July 2012).

World Health Organization (2008). *Policies and Practices for Mental Health in Europe – Meeting the challenges.* Copenhagen: WHO Regional Office for Europe. Available at: www.euro.who.int/__data/assets/pdf_file/0006/96450/E91732.pdf (accessed on 9 July 2012).

Zhou YY, Unitan R, Wang JJ, Garrido T, Chin HL, Turley MC, Radler L (2010). 'Improving population care with an integrated electronic panel support tool'. *Population Health Management*, vol 14, no 1, pp 3–9.